Unlimited Returns

Unlimited Returns
Your Blessing Guaranteed

"And prove me now herewith, saith the LORD of hosts,
if I will not open you the windows of heaven, and pour you out a blessing,
that there shall not be room enough to receive it . . ."

Emmanuel L. Amarteifio

Under the leadership of Bishop Dr. Susuana Amarteifio

authorHOUSE®

AuthorHouse™
1663 Liberty Drive
Bloomington, IN 47403
www.authorhouse.com
Phone: 1-800-839-8640

Published by AuthorHouse   05/29/2012

ISBN: 978-1-4685-8247-5 (sc)
ISBN: 978-1-4685-8246-8 (hc)
ISBN: 978-1-4685-8245-1 (e)

This book is a testament to the work of Bishop Dr. Susuana Amarteifio in the life of the author, Rev. Emmanuel L. Amarteifio, one of many leaders Bishop Susuana has raised in a lifetime of work in the Kingdom of God. Bishop Dr. Susuana Amarteifio has dedicated her whole life to God, making a difference in the lives of many, and raising leaders for the work of the Ministry wherever she goes.

She has travelled around the world and strongly believes that true leaders in Ministry do not delight in maintaining followers but raising leaders who will do greater works than they have done, and the best way to do that is by giving everybody a chance, to bring out the leader in them. This book is a testament to that philosophy. She is also the founder and leader of Jesus Christ of Nazareth International Church, with branches in Ghana, United Kingdom, Holland and Germany, and the author of *Destined for Excellence*.

"Return unto me and
I will return unto you,
Saith the LORD of hosts"

CONTENTS

DEDICATIONS

This book is dedicated to all those who are willing to return unto the LORD of hosts in Tithes and Offerings. May you find in Him all the things you are looking for in this life.

ACKNOWLEDGEMENTS

A message from Bishop Dr. Susuana Amarteifio:

"I give thanks to the Almighty God who called me into Ministry and has sustained me and given me a son in the Lord to produce this work. Thank you Lord for the life of Emmanuel, for the wisdom and knowledge you have given him, and for making this book not just a dream but also a reality.

Thanks to my husband Mr Napoleon Amarteifio and to all my children and grandchildren who have supported me all the way. And to my fellow Ministers who have remained faithful with me in the service of our Lord Jesus Christ till today, those in Ghana, the United Kingdom, the Netherlands and Germany, I say thank you and God bless you. Your labour in the Lord is not in vain.

To Apostle Enoch Okang Laryea and Rev. Mrs Helena Ayorkor Laryea, my backbone in Ministry; you started with me and you have remained faithful in the service of our Lord; I couldn't have made it without you.

To Apostle George Joshua and family, you have remained faithful and reliable for all these years, thank you.

To Apostle Albert Allotey, remain faithful, reliable and indispensable in the Ministry. You will be a light unto many and the Lord shall speak for you, God bless you.

To Apostle Joyce Dodoo and family, your dedication and service to the Lord will not go unrewarded. Those who sow in tears shall reap in joy. He who continually goes forth weeping, bearing seed for sowing, shall doubtless come again with rejoicing, bringing his sheaves with him.

To Apostle Gerald Thompson, may your hands be strengthened and may the Lord find you worthy, to entrust into your hands that which is your own according to his Word. It won't be long the whole world will hear about you and will glorify the Father in heaven.

To Apostle Nina Langlah and Rev Father Joe Mettle-Nunoo, I thank you for sacrificing all that you have in support of this Ministry. God will give you double.

To Rev. Emily Obiri-Yeboah, may the Lord satisfy you with long life and may your love for the Lord increase daily. The Lord knows your heart and your service to Him.

To Rev. Theresa Agyekum, Rev. Samantha Yeboah, my son Rev. David, Rev. Moses Sarquah, Rev. Moses Allotey, Rev-elect Kenny Akuffo Yirenkyi, Rev. Atta Owusu Antwi, and Rev. Naomi Ago, the Lord knows your work and He will reward you accordingly, may your strength in the Lord remain.

To Rev. Michael Lewis of Gomer Faith Ministries, may the Lord establish the work of your hands and may your Ministry prosper.

To Rev. Gabline Owusu-Boateng of Zion House Ministries, may your Ministry impact women. Adorn the incorruptible hearts of women with the ornament of a meek and quiet spirit, which is in the sight of God of great price. Beautify their spirits indeed and let the world behold their true nature.

To Rev. George and Dorcas Horatio-Larbie, may the Lord enlarge your territory, may doors of utterance be opened unto you worldwide. May the Lord establish the work of your hands.

To Archbishop J. P. Hackman (President of TAPAC), may the Lord make you great and establish the work of your hands. May your cup run over.

To Bishop Manasseh Antwi, Rev Rebecca Antwi, Bishop James Larbie, Rev Joan Larbie, Bishop Jonas Martinson, Apostle Faustina Clarke, Rev. Stella Lanfermann, Rev. Stella Matte, thank you for your partnership in the work of the Lord.

To all those who served with me in this Ministry in the past, and all those who helped and supported this Ministry in one way or the other, and to all those who have been there for me I say thank you and God bless you. Time and space will not permit me to mention all of your names".

FOREWORD

I have written this book for the generation of the 21ˢᵗ century and for the millions not yet born, to whom I have been called to serve. For your sake I have dedicated my life to search for the truth in all things so you can build yours on a solid rock. This book is for the one who wants to really get serious about success; I trust your life will never be the same again. If you are really **serious**, today will be your last day in whatever state of mind you may be in. A NEW MIND and a NEW HEART is coming to you, and it will be IMPOSSIBLE for you to fail in life, your SUCCESS is GUARANTEED.

Please read this book as many times as possible until you have taken in all the principles and made them yours. I know you will enjoy reading this book; it's nothing fancy, just straight to the point. I have discovered some truths with regards to the subject of Tithes and Offerings in relation to the great law of Cause and Effect, and I will like to share these with you. For every effect there is a cause, nothing happens by accident; there is a cause for Failure and there is a cause for Success. When your **daily thoughts are right** therefore, the effect will eventually be nothing short of Success in life. This book is also for those who need a strong basis for giving tithes and offerings in the 21st century. I shall update this book as I discover more truths about the subject. I beseech all pastors of local churches to recommend and encourage members of their congregation to read this book. I have communicated these truths in the simplest way possible so that anybody who reads can grasp and understand the truths without any difficulty.

Rev. Emmanuel L. Amarteifio (*Author*)

INTRODUCTION

There is but ONE source from which all things proceed; all the things we see and all the things we do not see was made by this All-Powerful source. Everything you will ever need in life, if they are not already here on earth, they are in this ONE source. He lives in all and He can influence all. In Him we all live and move and have our being.

I will attempt to bring your MIND in closer touch with this source, not just for a short moment but also for a lifetime. Success in life is what this book promises without fail, **if** you will **keep your MIND stayed on Him** from today and for the rest of your life. I can assure you that you will die a very HAPPY and a fulfilled person.

It does not matter how old you are, Success in life is still possible for you, if you will connect to this ONE source through what I'm about to share with you, and if you will KEEP YOUR MIND STAYED ON HIM everyday from morning till you go to sleep.

You are cordially invited to a lifetime of friendship with the "owner" of all the things you are looking for:

> "Return unto me,
> And I will return unto you":

R.S.V. P—The Lord God Almighty, "Possessor of Heaven and Earth"

The "Possessor of heaven and earth", the one who OWNS all the wealth of the nations invites you to this special relationship with Him. You will never regret it, if you will honour His invitation. There is so much to gain in this relationship and I suggest you consider it very carefully. Nobody loses in this relationship; it is a win–win situation. Return unto me and I will return unto you: this is a statement of psychological truth.

I intend to connect your MIND and keep it on the source of all the WEALTH and all the billions you may be looking for in life. For when your THOUGHTS are synchronised with His THOUGHTS daily, it will bring you nothing short of perfect peace of MIND, no matter what the circumstances, and you will attain an expected end, a very successful end indeed.

It will be impossible for you not to be successful in life if you will remain in the mental state that I am about to show you. It is the solid rock and the very foundation for true success. There are only three things I ask you to do: Fear God, Love Him and give Him GLORY for **everything**. That is to say, have **reverence** for God IN ALL THINGS and give the **GLORY** to Him FOR ALL THINGS 24 hours a day.

RETURN UNTO ME AND I WILL RETURN UNTO YOU

"**I am the LORD, I change not**;
Even from the days of your fathers ye are gone away from mine ordinances,
and have not kept them.
Return unto me, and I will return unto you, saith the LORD of hosts.
But you said, wherein shall we return?
Will a man rob God? Yet you have robbed me.
But ye say, wherein have we robbed thee?
In tithes and offerings.
You are cursed with a curse: **for you have robbed me**, even this whole nation.
Bring ye all the tithes into the storehouse, that there may be meat in mine house,
And prove me now herewith, saith the LORD of hosts,
If I will not open you the windows of heaven, and pour you out a blessing,
that there shall not be room enough to receive it.
And I will rebuke the devourer for your sakes,
And he shall not destroy the fruits of your ground;

Neither shall your vine cast her fruit before the time
in the field, saith the LORD of hosts.
And all nations shall call you blessed: for ye shall be a
delightsome land,
saith the LORD of hosts.

We shall discuss this fully in latter pages:

WISDOM IS THE PRINCIPAL THING

Solomon the wise king said: "Wisdom Is The PRINCIPAL Thing"; therefore GET WISDOM. It is the power to make good use of the knowledge of truth, without which you cannot be effective in any given task.

Again Solomon said: "in all your getting, get understanding". Without understanding, you will be doing what you feel is the right thing to do. It is always important to know 'WHY' you do the things you do. Getting the 'RIGHT PHILOSOPHY' is the key to doing things RIGHT in life.

Please allow me to start with the definition of KNOWLEDGE. Knowledge has been defined as 'organised' information in MIND: to have knowledge therefore, is the general awareness or possession of information, facts, ideas, truths, or principles. It is the awareness of information, either general or specific.

Knowledge is also defined as all that can be known: all the information, facts, truths, and principles learned throughout time. Information is the collected facts and data about a specific subject.

Even though wisdom is the most important thing to possess, it does not function in isolation. Wisdom only functions with Knowledge, (and by knowledge I mean, knowledge of truth not other people's opinion) and Understanding. Knowledge without Understanding is useless anyway; you will still be in the dark, there will be no light on your path. But here is the BIG one; Knowledge even with Understanding without WISDOM is 'NO GOOD' to you. You will never be able to rightly apply what you know without WISDOM, for Wisdom is the Power to apply knowledge rightly. That is why **Wisdom** is the **PRINCIPAL** thing. Let me say that again in many different ways:

> Wisdom is the **KEY** to all things!
> Wisdom is the **MAIN** THING!
> Wisdom is the **PRIMARY** THING!
> Wisdom is **MAJOR** in all things!
> Wisdom is the **CHIEF** THING!
> Wisdom is the **FOREMOST** THING!
> Wisdom is the **MOST IMPORTANT** THING!
> Wisdom is God working in you both TO WILL and TO DO of His good pleasure!
> Wisdom is the HOLY SPIRIT leading you in every step you take and in every move you make.
> Wisdom is God fully functional in your mind without any hindrance.
> Wisdom is the ability to discern the voice of the Holy Spirit and His leadings in all things.

So WHY IS WISDOM the Principal thing? Here is why: knowledge is only USEFUL when it is rightly applied, that's why wisdom is foremost and most important in all things. Without Wisdom, knowledge will not be useful or helpful to you at all in any way.

Observe doctors and some 'highly learned men' who smoke and drink alcohol heavily. They have all the knowledge that can be known, but THEY LACK WISDOM, 'the power'.

Even if you get ALL that can be known on a subject, and still lack the Wisdom to apply the knowledge, there will be no change in your situation, whatever the situation.

Attending Church services, Seminaries, Schools and Colleges, Seminars, Conferences. Breakfast Meetings etc, will only get you the right information you may be looking for, but the information must be rightly put into action, that's where Wisdom comes in.

The information in this book will NOT be useful or helpful to you at all if you do lack the Wisdom to apply it to your life. The effectiveness of this knowledge is in the **USE** and CORRECT APPLICATION thereof.

Again, there is but ONE source where all Wisdom comes from, and that is from above, from God Himself. You may at this juncture, say a short prayer to God, the Father, and ask for Wisdom with which to make wiser use of the knowledge contained in this book.

FATHER ABRAHAM'S GREATEST DISCOVERY

It all started when 'Father Abraham', after his return from the defeat of Chedorlaomer and the kings who were with him met Melchizedek whose name means King of Righteousness, the king of Salem or king of Peace, priest of the Most High God; and He blessed Abraham and said:

> "Blessed be Abram of God Most High, **Possessor of heaven and earth**;
> And blessed be God Most High, **who has delivered your enemies into your hand**."

When Abraham heard those words, he was struck in the heart, and his immediate reaction was this; he gave this King of Righteousness **a tithe of all**.

It is important that we investigate what happened to the **MIND** of Abraham? What caused him to give a tenth of all? Nothing will happen to your life until there is a **change in your MIND**. I'm afraid you will remain the same in every area of your life until there is a **CHANGE** in the MIND.

The words of Melchizedek, the Priest of the Most High God, addressed God as:

"Possessor of heaven and earth"

And that, this all-powerful God was the one who **"delivered the enemies into Abraham's hand"**

Now those words should strike the heart of anyone; to be informed that you are actually dealing with the OWNER of both Heaven and Earth, you must tremble with fear from the very core of your heart.

This KNOWLEDGE of truth is what I present to you in this book. When this knowledge **reaches your heart**, your reaction will be just as it was with Abraham; **a humble spirit will come upon you** and your attitude towards this "Possessor of heaven and earth" will change FOREVER.

You may now make a list of all the things you **really desire** to have as your possession here on earth. When you are finished, put the list aside, and continue reading this book. This book will hook you up with the **OWNER of ALL** the things you have just put on your list in a very HARMONIOUS way.

Let me continue with the story. After Abraham was enlightened with the knowledge that he was actually dealing with the Most High God ("**Possessor of heaven and earth**"), he made the FIRST MOVE; he started this beautiful relationship with the Most High God ("**Possessor of heaven and earth**"). For he thought to himself: 'if God gave me victory over a war that four kings and their army could not win, and if this God is really the "**Possessor of heaven and earth**", then *all that I have belongs to Him*. Not just that, but that *this God already possesses all the things I will ever need on this earth in my lifetime.* 'I might as well **initiate** a friendship with God right now'. And so with a humble spirit, with a heart of LOVE and of gratitude, he gave a TITHE of all.

If you would like to initiate this relationship with the ONE who possesses all the THINGS you listed on paper earlier, and more, all that I ask of you is to possess a HUMBLE spirit, a heart of LOVE and a heart of GRATITUDE.

Please allow me to stress a very important point here before I continue. Please do not confuse being a member of any local church, and perhaps paying your dues and tithes in that local church with THE BEAUTIFUL RELATIONSHIP you are about to forge with the "**Possessor of heaven and earth**". There are millions of people who go to church; most of them give Tithes and offerings and pay their local church dues alright, yet they have **no relationship** whatsoever with the "**Possessor of heaven and earth**", from whom all things come.

This knowledge has not entered into their hearts yet and so there is no **illumination** in their minds, without which they cannot attract God's attention 24 hours a day. They may be religious devout, members of a religious organisation, who may have entered into the Kingdom, but may be still at the door; they have still not yet possessed it. But Jesus said: "it is my Father's good pleasure to give you the Kingdom.

I can assure you that even some preachers who instruct you to give your tithes and offerings may NOT have understood the concept themselves and the effect it **MUST have on YOUR MIND** as a result of the relationship you establish with God, or they may be preaching it just to enrich their pockets.

I must say that going to church on Sundays to most people will soon become a useless religious activity if they still have no personal relationship with God and no UNDERSTANDING of the Kingdom of God on earth, that which Jesus Christ brought back to earth, preached about and paid the ultimate price of death on a cross for, so all may enter into. If you never establish that all-important one-to-one personal relationship with God, I'm afraid your Sunday church visits will be without a purpose other than to satisfy your 'addiction'; the habit you may have formed as a result of attending Church Services on Sundays, which you may have done for a long time since you were a little child.

Let me tell you a story that Jesus told, about this **'self justifying' and degrading mental attitude** of some churchgoers who may have no personal relationship with God at all:

> "Two men went up into the temple to pray; the one
> **a Pharisee**, and the other a publican. The **Pharisee**
> stood and **prayed thus with himself**:
> "God, I thank you, that I am not as other men are,
> extortioners, unjust, adulterers, or even as this publican.
> I fast twice in the week;
> **I give tithes of all that I possess.**

> And the publican, standing afar off, would not lift up
> so much as his eyes unto heaven, but smote upon his
> breast, saying, God be merciful to me a sinner.
> I tell you, this man went down to his house justified
> rather than the other: for every one that exalts himself
> shall be abased; and he that humbles himself shall be
> exalted.

Jesus calls such people hypocrites, for they do their charitable deeds before men, to be seen by them, that they may have **glory** from men. Jesus said, these people draw near to God with their mouth, and honour God with their lips, but **their hearts** are far from God. They teach as doctrines the commandments of men and **they worship God in vain**. They have reduced important spiritual activities such as fasting, prayer, giving of tithes and offerings and even the worldwide weekly worship services into **meaningless religious activities**.

You only have to observe such hypocrites for yourself; when they pray, they love to be seen 'in action'. They have some kind of spiritual techniques that make their prayers look very impressive to other 'folks' in the church. Their prayers are a mere recital of words; their **hearts** and **minds** are not in it, except in times of a desperate NEED FOR HELP. That's when they pray with all seriousness and make a connection with God in their hearts and minds. They are the ones who fill the seats of auditoriums and church premises across the world every blessed Sunday, wearing that 'God-fearing look on their faces' but their HEARTS are rotten, their MINDS are corrupt, and they drive people away from God by their negative attitudes. Their husbands and wives do not want to know about their church or God, and with time, their own children will cease to follow them to church. Their employers and bosses wonder what kind of God they claim to serve; for they are lazy at work, always late to work yet first to leave the office, slow at work, inefficient, unreliable, disrespectful, with bad attitude at work, insubordinate, not trustworthy. If their employers follow them to their homes, they will be shocked to see stuff they have stolen from their work places sitting in their homes as if they belong to them.

You cannot enjoy the real things of the kingdom until you UNDERSTAND how the Kingdom works. Something always happens to your **MIND** when **understanding** comes. That's what most people call a **paradigm shift**, because you literally walk into a new dimension of illumination. Your mental world changes completely, it sets you on a different mental path from most people, you **THINK differently**; things that worry most people worry you no more, you perceive things differently, you interpret situations and circumstances differently, you always see the 'good' in a bad situation, you react to situations differently, you do not recognise temporary failures, rather you use them as stepping stones to reach up higher. Your life becomes stress-free, and you will never again experience any kind of stress related disease, for your attitude changes completely, and you regain that ONE-TO-ONE, 'Father and son' relationship with God, which is able to make you CONFIDENT, FEARLESS, UNTOUCHABLE and truly RICH.

The wisdom in this book will set you on a path to develop a winning mental attitude. Never again will you panic even in the worst of situations, for you would have already hooked yourself up with the **"Possessor of heaven and earth"**. You don't even have to rush for things, neither should you compete for that which is already yours, for if 'All power' is on your side, you cannot fail. Your heart will remain steadfast, and you will not be moved by circumstances. Calmness of mind you will certainly enjoy, when your heart is filled with truth, and upon this truth your mind is fixed. When you are able to fix your mind upon truth alone, you cannot help but THINK about the truth in all circumstances, regardless of the appearances surrounding you. For in Him we live, and move and have our being.

This is the kind of **MIND** 'Father Abraham' developed as a result of that beautiful relationship he initiated with a **TITHE** at the words of the King of Righteousness, when he **realised** that the God in whom he has put his faith is actually the "**Possessor of heaven and earth**", which means that the God of Abraham is LORD both of heaven and earth. This light of revelation created a **NEW MIND** and a **NEW HEART** in Father Abraham. And this is the kind of NEW MIND and NEW HEART I want to present to you. This is exactly what I intend for this book to achieve in you.

Please read this book as many times as possible; you will then understand the principles, and may you receive a NEW MIND; a mind that God can work through to show Himself strong and mighty in you. Amen.

This New Mind you will obtain is an all-important factor in your special relationship with God, without which this relationship will be short-lived. This New Mind is a mind full of incredible faith in God, as the 'all potential' God, who is able to do anything. It is this kind of THOUGHT you must hold in your mind no matter what the circumstances. Always keep in mind that the God in whom you have put your faith is the "Possessor of heaven and earth". If you can think like this you will be fine, for God is more than able to move on the minds and hearts of men to bring you the things you need at the right time.

Coming into an AWARENESS of this truth, is but the beginning of this new journey into the discovery of a NEW world of possibilities. To summarise this in the words of Jesus, throughout this journey, "Have faith in God".

Let me say this to those who already give tithes and offerings to God. If the MENTAL conditioning necessary for this relationship is not there, I'm afraid there can be no relationship with the "Possessor of heaven and earth". This is why many religious people beg for things when they pray to God. Religion is a very hard work, but you don't have to go back to religion, you can make a 'U' turn today, and pursue 'this way'.

THE MODE OF TRANSACTION

The best way to THINK when doing business with your fellow man is this: "**as you would that men should do to you, do ye also to them likewise**". That is to say, deal with your fellow man fairly in every business transaction. **Do not get something for nothing; rather give to every man more than you take from him**.

Here is why: God deals with men in the same way. God always gives to every man MORE THAN He takes from him in the form of tithes and offerings. God is fair in doing business with all men.

WILL A MAN ROB GOD?

When you fail or refuse to bring God **Honour and Glory** for the things He freely gives you daily, you really HURT God's FEELINGS, **You actually ROB God of the Glory due to His name**.

ROBBING God of the Glory due to His name is a SERIOUS CRIME in the eyes of God. I call this a spiritual CRIME against God. I must warn you, anyone who tries to take God's Glory or even share in it, God will destroy; it is a great evil in the eyes of God.

Hear what God says concerning His glory:

> "I am the LORD: that is my name:
> and my glory will I not give to another,
> neither my praise to graven images".

Let me say that again in other words: God says, I am the OWNER of EVERYTHING, and nobody shares in my glory, the glory is all mine, all GLORY must be directed to me, and to me ALONE.

A bit of CAUTION here: now that you Understand what the 'Glory' means to God, you will have no excuse for failing to give Him what is due to Him

Please hear what God said to the chosen nation of Israel:

"Even from the days of your fathers you are gone away from mine ordinances, and have not kept them. **Return unto me, and I will return unto you**, saith the LORD of hosts. But ye said, **Wherein shall we return**?

Will **a man rob God**? Yet **you have robbed me**. But ye say, Wherein have we robbed thee? **In TITHES and OFFERINGS**.

Ye are cursed with a curse: for **you have robbed me, even this whole nation**.

Bring ye all the tithes into the storehouse, that there may be meat in mine house, and prove me now herewith, saith the LORD of hosts, if I will not open you the windows of heaven, and pour you out a blessing, that there shall not be room enough to receive it.

And I will rebuke the devourer for your sakes, and he shall not destroy the fruits of your ground; neither shall your vine cast her fruit before the time in the field, saith the LORD of hosts.

And all nations shall call you blessed: for you shall be a delightsome land, saith the LORD of hosts.

May the Holy Spirit give you a deeper revelation of His precious Word today.

David calls Him the King of Glory, and as King, He is also the Lord of Glory, which means that all glory in the heavens and in the earth belongs to Him and must be ascribed to His holy name.

GOD IS WORTHY TO RECEIVE THE GLORY

Now let me take you to heaven for a moment. The book of Revelations reveals the culture in heaven and it is a beautiful one there. According to John, in heaven they give God **GLORY** and **HONOUR** and **THANKS** all the time with their lips; and by falling on their faces before God in worship, or by casting down their crowns before the throne of Majesty. Whatever they do, they never fail nor cease to give GLORY to God. They say, God is worthy to receive ALL the GLORY, and the HONOUR and the POWER, for that is why He created all the things. They say God has created ALL THINGS just for **His PLEASURE**.

Do you see how the WILL of God is done in heaven, can you see how the people in heaven give God so much PLEASURE by giving Him GLORY and HONOUR and THANKS in all things continually? This is exactly what God is looking forward to, right here on earth; that in ALL things, we here on earth will give Him GLORY and HONOUR and THANKS. That is how God gets PLEASURE in all the things we do on earth. It pleases God so well when His WILL is done on earth. Any man who does the WILL of God on earth, God is well pleased with him.

It is the desire of God that ALL men will bring Him GLORY; He actually looks forward to it. That is why David said: "let everything that has breath, praise the Lord".

When you bring God your Tithes and Offerings, you Honour God, and when you Honour Him you bring Him GLORY, for you have acknowledged that, it is God who gives you power to get wealth. This in a nutshell is all God wants really from you, not your money, or produce. God doesn't need money; that is why He appoints men here on earth to receive these things on His behalf. God is only interested in your ATTITUDE of GRATITUDE, acknowledging the fact that He is the source of your wealth, even the source of your life, and by so doing, you bring Him GLORY.

Your tithe is the part of your increase that you sanctify and consecrate unto the Lord; it is this part that brings GLORY to the name of God. Whenever you bring God your tithes and offerings, you bring Him **HONOUR** and **GLORY**; this is why God invites everyone, individuals and businesses alike to do this honourable thing. God made it a law unto the people of Israel, but He wants you to do this with a better UNDERSTANDING and out of true LOVE and reverence for Him, acknowledging that it is God who gives you power to get wealth. The **GLORY** God gets when you do this honourable thing is what is more important to God, not your money. God has no need for things, He owns all things, and He is the possessor of the heavens and the earth. One day, all men will bring God glory.

"THE LORD GAVE"

The thing that kept Job going and sane in mind in his troubles was that he kept his MIND focused on the source of all things, God, the possessor of heaven and earth. Job's words were: "**the Lord gave**". Notice the state of his mind; it was focused on God, the source of all things. He acknowledged that everything he had, including his children and possessions, he "received" from the Lord. To Job, he was but a faithful steward.

When you UNDERSTAND that God is the source of ALL things, and that God first gave you ALL the things you already have, including your own life, it becomes easier to give unto Him your tithes and offerings.

This state of mind is more important than the things you have or will ever have, for to know that it is the Lord who gives, you keep your mind stayed on Him at all times, and whatever the circumstances, you will never be moved, for your faith is built on a "solid rock" that cannot be shaken. You can lean on Him and never be put to shame. God will indeed keep your mind in perfect peace, worry-free, because your mind is stayed on Him, and you know He is more than able to do exceedingly, abundantly above all that you can ever ask or think of, and there is NOTHING too hard for Him.

I say it again, people everywhere under the sun must practice this honourable thing; bring your tithes and offerings to God, the possessor of heaven and earth, so your **MIND** will be stayed on Him at all times and for all the things you will ever desire. When you bring your tithes and offerings unto God as a sign of obedience to the Law of Gratitude, it leaves a great effect on your mind; this effect on the mind is of great importance. *Nothing is more important than a mind, which is fixed on God, the creator*, the possessor of heaven and earth. That mind can achieve 'whatsoever things he desires'. David said: only fools say in their heart 'there is no God'.

PROVE ME

God is your source and sustainer, and in this He says, "**prove me**, find out for yourself, if I will not give you access to an open heaven. I will prove to you, that all the things you see come from me, and there is more where that came from". We as humans need food, water, clothing, shelter, love, good health and security, relationships etc. We depend on these 'things' for survival as human beings, and it seems as if whoever gives us these things to keep us going in this life, to him "we ascribe glory". In this God says prove me; find out for yourself if "I am not the one who truly gives all things you desire". You will discover that all these people and gods to whom you give glory are usurpers. None of the glory and honour you continually give to them belongs to them. All the glory and honour belongs to God.

You always rob God of his glory, the glory due to Him. You deprive God of the glory which is rightfully His, and you give it to men and little gods made of wood and stone by the hands of men. Even though you know that robbery is a crime anywhere on the face of the earth, you chose not to rob from men but from God, "the Possessor of heaven and earth". How huge a crime do you think "robbing God" is? What do you think the penalty for such huge crime must be? You be the judge.

How would you know if I am lying about all that I have written in this book if you don't prove it for yourself, exactly the way I have passed it on to you? This whole world is His idea in the first place, what makes you think he will leave you without any good thing. All He asks of you is to give Him your **mind** again, you take the first step, bring the glory which belongs to Him, keep your Mind on Him, let Him fill your thoughts, do not allow any other thoughts to interfere with this in your mind. Keep your focus on Him, even in times when things seem to be going in the wrong direction. **Don't doubt Him for a second**, He has a mind better than yours, a mind that knows what's about to happen to you tomorrow. Give thanks for all things, and watch Him do the rest.

YOUR TITHES

Giving God your tithes and offerings is doing SERIOUS BUSINESS with God. God desires all men to bring Him GLORY, because He is worthy to receive it, He deserves all Glory, all Glory belongs to Him; you must bring ALL glory to Him. **It is your DUTY to give unto the LORD the glory due to His name.**

In your business dealings with men, you must 'give to every man that which belongs to him'. In the same way, you MUST give to God THAT WHICH BELONGS TO HIM. When you bring your tithes and offerings to God, you **'honour God'**; you acknowledge that it is God who has given you the power to get wealth, in this way **'you give God the glory due His name'**; this Glory, He shares with no man and no other god.

And God will not take from you something without giving you back what belongs to you. Remember He is fair in dealing with all men.

When you give God this kind of **high respect**, He will also have to give you back that which belongs to you. He will always give back to you that which belongs to you, and this is called '**the Blessing**'. This is why the man who stands in the place of God to receive your tithes **MUST bless you in the name of the Lord**. The man or woman who stands in the place of God here on earth as in the case of Melchizedek, must be one who stands high above you spiritually, as ordained by God Himself, one you can submit to, and to whom it is also **proper** to hand over your tithes; one who can receive your tithes on behalf of God, and is also in the position by **God's own standards**, to **bless you in an orderly manner**, according to the Scriptures.

When '**the blessing**' is pronounced on you, it is worth a million times more than the substance you brought to God, for they include **everything** you can ever ask for.

When God instructed Moses to tell Aaron and his sons the exact words to speak when they bless the children of Israel, He knew exactly what He was doing, for those words include everything; perfect peace of mind, physical health, grace and mercy, protection from danger, favour and material wealth. God said: put my name upon the children of Israel, and I will bless them.

> "The LORD bless you, and keep you:
> The LORD make his face shine upon you, and be
> gracious unto you:
> The LORD lift up his countenance upon you, and
> give you peace".

When Melchizedek, king of Salem, priest of the most high God, met Abraham returning from the slaughter of the kings, **He blessed** Abraham in the name of the Lord, "Possessor of heaven and earth", and Abraham gave a **tenth part of all** to him as one who stands in the place of God to receive tithes on behalf of God.

Here is the Key:"and without all contradiction, the **less is blessed of the better**". It is God who has arranged it this way, that all will be able to relate to Him in the matter of giving of Tithes and Offerings.

God will always appoint men to stand in His place to receive the tithes so they will bless you in His name. This is why even the priests who receive tithes on behalf of God, MUST also submit to a higher authority (other men of God whom God has placed over them as a spiritual covering/authority), to whom they must give their tithes and offerings so they too will receive the **blessing**. Nobody is exempted from this beautiful relationship with God, for ALL must look upwards to God; everyone must be connected to the source of all things, **everybody NEEDS the BLESSING which comes from God,** for it is the blessing of the Lord which makes a man truly rich, NOT HARD WORK.

SUBMISSION TO SPIRITUAL AUTHORITY IS GOD'S IDEA

Submission to spiritual authority is God's idea even if some men of God for the wrong reasons corrupt the idea. I am aware that there are corrupt men of God out there who abuse their positions; some misappropriate the resources of God; others preach about tithes and offerings, not for God, not for your sake, but for their own gain. But you need not worry your head over them. You have believed in a principle that works for eternity and that's all you have to keep in mind. There have been corrupt men of God in the past, and it is very unlikely that there will not be many more corrupt men of God in the future. These men are like corrupt government officials; you always find them in every government; they bring nothing but shame to the name of God. Some may be in your own church, but they have their own problems to deal with.

Do not let such negative thoughts interfere with what you now hold in your mind as truth. You have responded to God's invitation, it is to God you give your tithes and offerings, not man. You must retain this in your mind always, so you can firmly fix your mind on God, looking up only to God, the source of all things for 'whatsoever things your heart desires'.

God is a Spirit, and as a Spirit, He lives in a different world; heaven, an invisible world, where God reigns as King. He does not live in houses made by the hands of men, He does not use our monies, He does not drink grape juice, He has no use for your cars, He does not need your crops, He does not personally use any of the things you bring Him as tithes and offerings because He is a Spirit. However, since the days of Abraham, God had made a wonderful arrangement for the receiving of tithes and offerings. He has set up human agencies all over the world, whom He has set apart, ordained and 'Authorised' to receive the tithes on His behalf, so that He can keep this beautiful relationship He has established with mankind. God desires for all men to set their minds upon Him in all things. He wants you to fix your mind on Him constantly so He will be your **all in all**, to **live and move and have your being in Him ALONE**. This is very, very important to God. **This, right here is the heart of this book**. This is the very reason why God hates it when you put your trust in another man or when you go to other gods, giving glory to them as if they care more about you than God; as if God is an irresponsible Father. So whether God blesses you **indirectly** by causing men to give to you the things you desire, or **directly** without the need for other humans to play the middleman between you and God, like when Manna falls from heaven directly to you, or the rain pouring down on your land, or the sun shining brightly so you can see clearly in the day, or the air you breathe coming to you directly without the need for human agencies to partake in the delivery process, KNOW THAT IT IS GOD who supplies all your needs according to His riches in glory. If you understand this, you will be able to give God all the glory and thanks for ALL THINGS.

If God claims that the whole earth belongs to Him, and that all the worlds and everything in it also belong to Him, and if the highest heavens and the invisible worlds also belong to Him; **won't you like to relate to this God in a 'Harmonious' way**, as He is very well able to move on the hearts of every man, no matter how far they live from you; and He is able to influence people to bring you all that your heart desires for better living and fuller life? He is even able to send angels down from the invisible heaven to you right where you are, to bring you a word that will change your life for good.

BRINGING YOUR TITHES UNTO GOD

When God the Father is given the glory in heaven, it gives Him so much pleasure, more than anything else you can ever offer him.

To give one tenth of all your increase is basic mathematics but must be taken seriously. This means, you MUST KNOW what the **total sum** is, before you give **one tenth**. It should not be guesswork at all; it MUST be done with mathematical certainty. You cannot treat this casually, you cannot be lazy in this work; you cannot just give God any amount as your tithes. You have to be mindful of all the things God gives you daily, otherwise you will not be able to give Him Thanks for **all things;** neither will you be able to give Him ALL the GLORY that is **due** to His Holy Name.

If you really want to maintain your relationship with God in the giving of Tithes and offerings, then **you must keep accurate records of all** that God gives you; that is how you will be able to give exactly one tenth of it to God. You must be serious with God in this matter.

Please remember you are dealing with the Possessor of heaven and earth, the Lord of heaven and earth, the owner of all things visible and invisible, the God who has numbered the very hairs on your head. He is accurate and precise in the things he does. Look around you and you will agree with me that He does all things **decently** and **in order**, and so must you.

Even for the ungodly, to maintain a good relationship with their governments, they keep accurate records of all their earnings. The rich man who can afford the services of accountants, hire them to keep their books correctly for them, in order that they don't appear to be evading taxes by keeping bad records of all their taxable earnings. By this, they are able to pay every amount of tax due to their governments, thereby maintaining a right standing with their governments. If the ungodly is wise enough to do this, then you cannot treat God any less.

HONOUR THE LORD WITH YOUR SUBSTANCE

There is a Law of Gratitude, and anyone who obeys this law will enjoy the benefits thereof; by law, not by chance. The mental attitude of gratitude draws the mind into a closer touch with God, the possessor of heaven and earth. The spiritual exercise of gratitude alone, backed by the actual giving of your tithes and offerings unto God faithfully and reverently, will keep your mind fixed on God, the source from which all things come.

Bringing your tithes and offerings unto God is in obedience to this Law of Gratitude. When you trust in the Lord with all your heart, leaning NOT on your own understanding, **total peace of mind**, even in the midst of trouble, will be your reward. For all those who trust in the LORD, are like Mount Zion, which cannot be moved, but abides forever. No circumstance can move you, and nothing shall by any means rob you of your peace of mind.

Here is Solomon's wisest counsel when it comes to giving unto the Lord: "**Honour the LORD with your substance** or possessions, and with the first fruits of all your increase". No need to tell you why, for without God, it is in vain for you to rise up early, and sit up late, to eat from the sweat of your brow. Without God, you will always have to 'work hard' for things. Your life will be a very stressful one. But God gives His beloved sleep, they lie down in bed and they are never afraid; their sleep is always sweet. Solomon said if you honour the Lord with your substance, the Lord will in turn cause your barns to be filled with plenty, and your vats will overflow with new wine. In this, God says, '**prove me**'; discover for yourself if this statement is true or not; there is nothing to lose in this relationship, absolutely NOTHING. Here is the truth you need to retain in your mind: '**it is the LORD your God, who gives you power to get wealth**'

When you fail to relate yourself to God through the giving of Tithes and Offerings, your focus, your attention and your mind shifts from God as the SOURCE of all things, to yourself and others or even idols. You lean on your own strength and on the strength of others, and you put your trust in 'other gods' fashioned by the hands of men for the things you need and want in life. And you may say in your heart: 'my power and the might of my hand have gained me this wealth.'

Whenever you bring your tithes and offerings to God, it's like you give God the green light to make a forward movement towards you, and you know God will always give you back **much more** than you can EVER give to Him. The law of sowing and reaping goes to work for you, just as a farmer sows little but reaps much, so will God do unto you. Jesus said: when you g**ive, it shall be given unto you**, in good measure, pressed down, and shaken together, and running over, shall men give into your bosom. For with the same measure that ye mete withal it shall be measured to you again. A new world will unfold itself to you, "where it is more blessed to give than to receive."

Giving your Tithes to God is giving upward, **to God**; this keeps your MIND focused on God, looking upward unto God alone, not man. Your expectations and your faith must be towards God, for every good gift and every perfect gift comes from above, and they come down from the Father who created the sun and the moon and the stars.

This truth is important because 'Wisdom' only works with the knowledge of truth. So **until** you find **truth** in your knowledge, wisdom cannot help you. Take every opportunity to **renew your mind daily in the knowledge of TRUTH**, because your MIND is a very important part of your being without which God cannot accomplish His purposes on earth through you. It is the way you condition your mind that keeps you great or small; it is the way you THINK that makes you bold or afraid of circumstances.

The law of sowing and reaping works for you if you are a **giver**; farmers always sow in hope, they always expect a harvest when they sow, they sow a little, but they always reap in abundance, and the more they sow, the more they reap; farmers understand this as an eternal principle which does not change. Make this principle work for you; he who sows bountifully shall also reap bountifully, and he who sows sparingly shall reap likewise.

It does not matter how much you give to God, He knows the value of your gift. It may look small in value to you, but God sees your heart and He knows the true value of your gift to Him. But remember, God loves a cheerful giver.

There is but ONE law under the sun, to which all men must submit, and this is the 'Law of LOVE'. It is the law that compels your heart to share your bread with the man who has no bread to eat. It is the law that worketh in you to do of God's good pleasure. It is the same Law of Love that makes you want to share all that you possess with others; with the poor and needy too, even to the extent of giving of your own life, talents and gifts for the benefits of others.

This same Law of Love MUST motivate the giving of your Tithes and Offerings, which you bring to God faithfully and reverently. Give to God because you love Him. Express your LOVE for Him freely everyday **with the seal of your GIFT**, in honour of His holy name, and in appreciation of his manifold blessings towards you; even for the life that you have. Anyone who follows this simple instruction will personally attract God to himself, that's a promise. Your mind will be constantly stayed on God, and God will keep your MIND in "perfect peace", and NOTHING shall by any means move you.

Giving your tithes is one sure way of acknowledging God in your daily life and as a sign of Gratitude. It is as essential to God as paying your taxes is to your government. God has a plan for the use of tithes, so failing or refusing to bring Him your tithes does not only show ingratitude towards God for the bountiful supplies he has already given you, even for the breath of life that you still enjoy so you can live to make more of such wealth, but you also attempt to disrupt God's program designed for the administration of the Tithes and Offerings.

For those who are waiting to be mega rich before they start giving, here is a word from Jesus: "He that **is** faithful in that which is least **is** faithful also in much. Please note the word **IS**; it's in the present tense. **IS,** not **will be**—so START GIVING to God NOW.

Jesus also says; "he that is unjust in the least is unjust also in much". If therefore ye have not been faithful in the unrighteous mammon, **who will commit to your trust the TRUE RICHES**?

There is more, so much more than money or things that God has in store for you. There are business ideas, projects, books, inventions, technologies that the world has never known and great works that God actually wants to commit to your trust; there is so much more than you can ever imagine. Possibilities are UNLIMITED with God.

HAVING THE RIGHT ATTITUDE

Let me continue with the story of Abraham: the only reason why Abraham went to war was to save his nephew and that was it. There was no other agenda on his mind. He had no interest in the goods of Sodom, for he did not go to war for gain. However, after he had rescued his nephew by the HELP of God, he was also able to retrieve all the goods of Sodom and Gomorrah that their captors took away from them. When Abraham came back and after he had initiated his **deeper relationship** with the "Possessor of heaven and earth", by giving his Tithe, the king of Sodom said to Abraham, "Give me the persons, and take the goods for yourself. Remember, the goods Abraham brought back **belonged to** the King and the people of Sodom and Gomorrah. This was the reply of Abraham to the king of Sodom:

> "I have raised my hand to the LORD, God Most High, the Possessor of heaven and earth, that I will take nothing, from a thread to a sandal strap, and that **I will not take anything that is yours**, lest you should say, 'I have made Abram RICH'".

When Abraham gave **tithe** to the High Priest of God, something happened to his **mind** instantly. He connected his **MIND instantly** to the invisible source of all things, and even though he had not yet received so much from God, but for his expectations of God, who is the invisible, inexhaustible source of ALL THINGS, being able to make him RICH, he REFUSED to take the goods and possessions of the Kings of Sodom and Gomorrah, for he wanted NOTHING that does not belong to him. Those things belonged to the King and the people of Sodom so he wanted none of that. He only went to war to save his nephew, not for gain. Abraham believed God's inexhaustible supply was able to make him truly RICH, and this **expectation** alone became his **FAITH.**

This is exactly what will happen to your MIND when you establish this beautiful relationship with God, through the giving of your Tithes and Offerings. Your **MIND** will be constantly "stayed on God". You will not be in haste to get rich, you will not need to take shortcuts, you will have no need to defraud your fellow man, you will not have to step on people's toes to promote yourself for promotion comes from God (and you want to relate to Him in a harmonious way). You do not want anything that belongs to another man, for you will be dealing with the living God, the possessor of heaven and earth who giveth us richly all things to enjoy.

It is very important that you discern the **CHANGE** that occurred in the **MIND** of Abraham? He refused to take a **shortcut** to riches by taking goods which **belonged to someone else**. He believed that, the one in whom He has BELIEVED, is indeed "the Possessor of heaven and earth". And if He is, then there can be NO SHORTAGE of THINGS with Him in the invisible world of God, where ALL THINGS come from.

This is an **important change** that **MUST** happen to you in the **MIND** if you decide to take this surest route to SUCCESS. There are **no shortages** in the world of the invisible God, in whom you have believed. The whole world belongs to Him, He can move on the hearts of men, many miles away from where you are right now, to bring to you "**whatsoever things your heart desires**". This is the ONLY reason why you MUST LOOK UP in all things to God in prayer, for all the things your heart desires, and maintain that harmonious relationship with Him, other than putting your trust in men or cutting corners or even begging for things.

Here is what you need to remember; as you agree to establish a relationship with the ORIGINAL SOURCE of ALL THINGS, **you do not want to have that which belongs to another man**. You do not want to covet another man's stuff; all you seek for is "whatsoever things your heart desires". When those mental pictures of "whatsoever things your heart desires" are clearly formed in your mind, express them to God (the "Possessor of heaven and earth") in prayer. And you let your FAITH do the rest; hold on to them by faith, that they are coming to you, **until** you receive them.

You MUST look upward to God **everyday**, for all the things you desire; Jesus said, we MUST LOOK UPWARD to our **Father in heaven** for "**our DAILY bread**"; that includes everything that pertains to life and godliness in EACH DAY. Never trust the things you have, only **TRUST the God you have**; He remains the same forever. When you depend on God and NOT on THINGS or PEOPLE, your 'every day' MUST be a successful one. If you depend on the things you already have, especially if you are a bit loaded with cash and property, it may fail you most of the time.

You are destined for greatness. Never lose your faith in God. Be confident about this: God believes in you, so believe in yourself. And if 'All-Power' (God) is working with you, it will be impossible for you to fail. Do not despise humble beginnings, for God is no respecter of persons; it doesn't matter what your background or level of education may be or whether you have little or much today. If you will take charge of your life today and go to work with God, He will surely bring you to an expected end, for God created you to be successful in your calling.

IT IS YOUR MIND THAT KEEPS YOU SMALL

It is your MIND that keeps you small; it is the attitude of your mind that determines your response to circumstances. In **the mind** of the widow of Zarephath, all she had was but a handful of meal in a barrel, and a little oil in a cruse and she was gathering two sticks that she may go in and dress it for herself and her son that they may eat it, and **die**. She was not aware of the invisible, inexhaustible provision and supplies from anywhere else apart from what she had in her possession. Her source of supply was limited and so she willingly expected death to come when their last meal was consumed.

This is the case for many people, they live and depend on their paycheques other than God for life, so their supply is limited, they are reduced to their monthly paycheques; they cannot do anything beyond that. They look at their paycheques and say to themselves, "that is all there is". Their budgets are tight, for they cannot **believe** beyond what they receive from employers. I tell you the truth, FAITH in God, is the highest virtue one can ever attain, and this virtue is a function of the MIND.

The widow of Zarephath was heading for the worst until Elijah showed up and redirected her **mind** towards the Possessor of heaven and earth, the source where all things come from, and when she **believed**, her attitude changed, even death could not visit her that day. What a difference this makes in life; what a change in attitude, when your mind is firmly fixed on the source of all things, when your faith is in God.

People who live without a **living faith**, have an attitude like that of the widow of Zarephath before Elijah met with her. What they see with their physical eyes is to them "all there is". They have no connection with the source of all things; their minds are only fixed on people (friends, employers, family members etc) and the things they receive from them. They have no **faith in God**, they cannot believe beyond what they see with their eyes, they give up too soon, for there is no HOPE for them and they gladly invite death to come.

Great men detach their hearts and minds from things; they have learned to live with little and to live with much. Their minds are constantly fixed on the source of all things, not things. Things no longer rule their minds. Of course they feel pain, hurts and disappointments like everybody else, but they do not allow their feelings to rule their minds. It is your response to situations that matters, not the situation itself.

WHATSOEVER THINGS YOU DESIRE

The path you are about to set foot on is really full of unlimited possibilities. Let me quote an authority on the subject; Jesus Christ Himself:

> "Therefore I say unto you, **whatsoever things** you desire,
>
> When you **pray, believe that you receive them**, and **you shall have them**".
>
> "**Whosoever** shall say unto this mountain, be thou removed, and be thou cast into the sea; and shall **not doubt** in his heart, but shall **believe** that those things which he saith **shall come to pass**; **he shall have whatsoever he saith**.

Note the words of Jesus carefully:

1. There is NO LIMIT on the things that you may desire, "**whatsoever things**". The only limit is with your ability to desire. Certainly not of desiring vain things, for ungodly people do that.

2. You do not have to keep repeating the same prayer over and over. Jesus said it is not in the repetition of your words that gets your prayer requests across. Heathens do that, for **they**

THINK that they will be heard for their many words. But your Father knows the things you have need of before you ask Him.

3. What is MORE IMPORTANT is this: all you need to do is to "believe that you receive them". Hold them in your thoughts as though they were with you in the physical realm. Talk about them as though they are here with you. Think about them as though they are on their way, and they are coming to you when you are ready to receive them. Act and take on the attitude as though you already have them. This may sound ridiculous, as most men want to see before they believe. This is ACTIVE FAITH. This kind of faith is an **Intangible Substance** yet real, except that this substance cannot be seen with your physical eyes. And you only talk about it as though they were, for of a truth, THEY ARE. They are your earnest expectations, you hold on to them in YOUR MIND until they manifest in the physical realm for all to see. This mental exercise is of immense importance. The more you are able to do this the greater your faith will be, and the greater your faith, the MORE THINGS you can draw from the INVISIBLE and INEXHAUSTIBLE world of God, (the **"Possessor of heaven and earth"**), where ALL THINGS come from.

The principles I have laid down in the above statements have been tried and tested, not only by me, but also by greater men past and present. I will emphasise a bit more on the third one, **"believe that you receive them**, and you shall have them. This is not a mental exercise in vain. This ACTIVE FAITH ALONE will get you ALL THE THINGS, "whatsoever you desire". It is the sure way of getting your prayers answered. It is the surest way of forging a stronger bond in your relationship with the "Possessor of heaven and earth.

You may ask: for how long am I supposed to wait? Well, for the people on the fast lane to riches, this may not work for you at all. Your mental attitude of impatience, doubt and unbelief will interfere and quickly shut down any progress you are making on this path. It seems to be the hardest work in the world; to be able to hold on to the TRUTH in your mind, to keep the faith, **when all the circumstances and things surrounding you seem to be going in the opposite direction.** When your illness does not seem to be getting any better, when you lose your job and the bailiffs come knocking on your door, when creditors are chasing you for their money, when your rent is due and there is not enough food to eat at home for you and for your children, and the balance on your bank account is in the red, when your utility bill payments have fallen behind, when your children's school fees have not been fully paid and your mortgage lenders are threatening to repossess your house. HOW LONG ARE YOU SUPPOSED TO WAIT?

Let me answer you in the words of a more qualified person than myself: Job who lived a few thousand years ago said, "all the days of my appointed time will I wait, **TILL MY CHANGE COME**". There is no giving up UNTIL there is a CHANGE in your situation or circumstances. You want a Living Faith, not a dead one.

Unwavering Faith in the face of uncertainty is the ONLY sure way to OVERCOME the fiery darts of **FEAR**, doubts and their allies, being shot at you in the MIND. One shot of doubt entertained in the **MIND** can shut down the whole process of receiving by faith from the unseen world, where ALL the things you desire MUST come from.

If you want to know whether it was worth it for Job to WAIT, holding on to his FAITH for however long it took for his change to come, here it is: "the LORD gave Job **twice** as much as he had before, all his brethren, and all his sisters, and all they that had been of his acquaintance before, and did eat bread with him in his house, every man also gave him a piece of **money,** and every one an earring of **GOLD**. So the LORD *blessed the latter end of Job more than his beginning*: for he had fourteen thousand sheep, and six thousand camels, and a thousand yoke of oxen, and a thousand she asses. He had also seven sons and three daughters. And in all the land were no women found so fair as the daughters of Job. After this, Job lived an hundred and forty years, and saw his sons, and his sons' sons, even four generations. So Job died, being old and full of days.

Let me say this: God works with our desires and decisions, and by desires, I mean that which you are so passionate about, that which you are willing to pay the full price for. It is the kind of desire with an attitude of 'I won't quit till my change comes', for you cannot move the hand of God towards you by casual faith. So whatever your heart's desires may be, whatever God lays on your heart to do, whether you have enough resources or not, make the decision, go for it, and God will back your every move. God will send you all the help you will need on the way, to fulfill your heart's desires, be it intellectual help, human resources, financial help, or spiritual help. Unless you make that crucial decision to go for it, God will not move towards you. This is a practical life of faith, for the just shall live by his faith.

Whatever your heart's desires may be, start working on them now, don't delay, God is waiting on you, He is waiting to direct your steps, **but you need to plan your way, set the goal and He will direct your steps**. He knows the troubles ahead of you, and He will surely deliver you from all evil. He will not allow your foot to be moved. He is your keeper, He does not slumber nor sleep, He will not allow the evil one to come near your dwelling, He shall preserve your soul, He will preserve your going out and your coming in until you succeed. He will find you wise counsel to establish all your plans for He knows where all the help you need may be found.

Whatever your goals may be, do not hesitate to write them down so you can remind yourself daily; make plans to achieve them, and work on those plans every single day. This is what YOU MUST DO; God will certainly do his part as He promised. Please do not fail to do your part, for God desires to work WITH you, not without you. If you follow this simple advice, it would be more valuable to you, and it would be of more help to you than anything else you could ever learn in any top University in the world. You will soon find yourself working in a harmonious way with the "owner of heaven and earth"; and this will certainly change your life for good. I am looking forward to millions of people testifying to this truth, people of this generation and millions more not yet born, to whom I have been called to serve.

And now let us deal with the phrase "**whatsoever things you desire**". I made an important discovery, that when Jesus says: "whatsoever things you desire", he is talking about your **ability to will 'The Will of God' in all things;** to "desire" in accordance with the Will of God. That is to say, everything you desire must please God, for God

ONLY works in you to will and to do of His good pleasure. Nothing LESS! Any "desire" other than that which will bring God pleasure is not from God, and if it is not from God, He cannot be the one responsible for giving you those things. Remember, the relationship you want to establish with God has to be a **harmonious** one. If all your desires are not in the 'Will of God', your relationship with Him will not last. All things that God does must first give Him pleasure; so check your "desires" to see if they will give God pleasure. Ask yourself; is this desire in the will of God? Is it going to give God all the glory? If God should check the list of your desires and ask Himself: "what's in it for me", would He find "glory" in your "desires" at all? Jesus said: "that men may see your good works and glorify your Father in Heaven". God MUST get glory for every 'good' work done under the sun.

If God gets no glory in your desires, petitions and requests made unto Him, He does not grant those desires. And if He does not grant them, **who does**? Please make this note: Everything God does, is counterfeited by the wicked world of darkness where Satan rules as the Prince of darkness. So for example, if Mr Brown says to himself: "I desire for my boss to be fired that I may be put in charge, to take his place"; if Mr Brown is able to form a clear mental picture of what he has desired, and if he expresses this thought by the word of mouth or by prayer, and if he holds this thought (that clearly formed mental picture) in his mind, and believes strongly in his heart that he will get what he has desired; if he goes to work and sees himself as one who will soon replace his boss at work, and if he keeps talking about it as though it has come to pass, if begins to act and do things like a boss in his mind so that his daily expectation is about this one thing; if he never lets go of this idea he has conceived in his mind, he may eventually get his boss 'fired', and it is very likely that he will take the place of his boss, ONLY that, this kind of answer to prayer or "things you desire" does not come from God.

Sometimes you wonder why the ungodly get things done for them and much quicker too, even though their minds are corrupt and their desires are all ungodly. The dark world of wickedness counterfeits the ways, principles and methods of God. There is a clear difference between good and evil: Good always brings glory to God, evil doesn't.

There is a certain way to think and act in order to get things done for you in the spiritual world; that is why the ungodly too become "successful" in their wicked thoughts. Yes, they do get results; BUT God is NOT in their THOUGHTS and God is not pleased with them. Riches gained by this method are feverish, full of sorrows and do not last, for God is NOT in it. It is the BLESSING of the Lord that makes one truly rich and He adds no sorrow with it.

It really hurts to see the wicked "prosper"; armed robbers and thieves riding in the best cars, drug dealers living in the finest houses, corrupt government officials owning and running big companies and industries, crooks running big enterprises, murderers owning large sums of money in the bank, fraudulent men seem to get ahead in life, even 'corrupt **men of God**' running mega churches. It makes you wonder, is there any justice in this life? Well, you are not alone.

The psalmist thought of this evil in the land of the living, and complained to God. He sought to understand why this is so, why God permits such injustices to go on in this world. Then he made an amazing discovery that changed his THINKING forever, and he rested his mind. Let me share this with you so you too don't get frustrated, please keep going in the right direction:

"Truly God is good to such as are pure in heart.
But as for me, my feet had almost stumbled;
My steps had nearly slipped.
For I was envious of the boastful, when I saw the prosperity of the wicked.
For there are no pangs in their death, but their strength is firm.
They are not in trouble as other men, nor are they plagued like other men.
Therefore pride serves as their necklace; violence covers them like a garment.
Their eyes bulge with abundance; they have more than heart could wish.
They scoff and speak wickedly concerning oppression; they speak loftily. They set their mouth against the heavens, and their tongue walks through the earth.
Therefore his people return here, and waters of a full cup are drained by them.
And they say, "How does God know? And is there knowledge in the Most High?"
Behold, these are the ungodly, who are always at ease; they increase in riches.
Surely I have cleansed my heart in vain, and washed my hands in innocence.
When I thought how to understand this, **it was too painful for me**;

Until I went into the sanctuary of God; then **I understood their end**.

Surely You set them in slippery places; you cast them down to destruction.

Oh, how they are brought to desolation, as in a moment!

They are utterly consumed with terrors. As a dream when one awakes,

So, Lord, when You awake, You shall despise their image.

Thus my heart was grieved, and **I was vexed in my mind**.

I was so foolish and ignorant; I was like a beast before You.

Nevertheless I am continually with You; You hold me by my right hand.

You will guide me with Your counsel, and afterward receive me to glory.

For indeed, those who are far from You shall perish; You have destroyed all those who desert You for harlotry.

But **it is good for me to draw near to God**; I have put my trust in the Lord GOD".

The BIG difference between you and the ungodly man who seem to 'prosper' can be summarised in the words of Solomon:

"the end of a thing is better than its beginning".

This is a very important statement you must keep in your heart all the days of your life,

Worry yourself no more about such people, and do not be tempted to follow the ungodly in their evil thoughts and ways. God is the one supplying you with riches, so do not be envious of them; do not compare yourself to them. Desire your own wealth, and pursue it with all your heart and mind and strength. God gets NO GLORY in the prosperity of the wicked, for He is NOT in their THOUGHTS.

WHAT THE GREAT MEN HAD IN COMMON

All the great men we know in history, past and present were and are men of faith. **Faith** is the most distinguishing factor that they all possessed in varying degrees. If you ask the great man Moses how he intended to find food and water for the people he was leading from the land of slavery into the promised land, for both children, women and men, his reply would be, "**I don't know** but God will provide"

May be so many lives depend on you today, I beseech you to learn the lesson right here in the above paragraph if you are going to achieve any measure of greatness in life, God's way.

Let me tell you more about Abraham and what happened to his **mind** and the change in his **attitude** towards God (the Possessor of heaven and earth), because this is exactly what will eventually happen to you in this beautiful relationship you are about to establish with God. **You will be fearless**, and your faith and hope will be in God, and you will soon believe God to do for you the things that seem IMPOSSIBLE to others, and you will be living in a different world.

> Now God said to Abraham: "Take your son, your only son, Isaac, whom you love, and go to the region of Moriah. Sacrifice him there as a burnt offering on one of the mountains I will tell you about."

When you are at the age of Abraham, a man over 100 years old, you will understand that NOTHING is more important to you at that stage in life than to ensure the life of the ONE who will SUCCEED you. So the instruction of God to sacrifice His son, the promised child, the successor of Abraham, was like a heavyweight PUNCH on his face. He will be left with NOTHING if Isaac is sacrificed, back to zero. It means he will have to start all over again, believing God for another son by Sarah who is also very old.

Even in the toughest trials of your faith, do what Abraham did; don't stop **believing** in the **TRUTH**. God had already said to Abraham: "I have made you a father of many nations", so it was up to Abraham to **believe** this WORD, which came out of the mouth of God. Abraham had already witnessed with his eyes what God did with the womb of Sarah his wife, for God brought the dead womb back to life; Sarah's womb was able to conceive a child in a very old age, well past menopause. So he believed God, who gives life to the dead and calls those things, which do not exist as though they are. **Contrary to hope, in hope he believed**, and that's how he became the father of many nations, according to what God had spoken concerning him.

When you give your tithes and offerings to God, God promises to give you "**access to an open heaven**", but NOTHING will fall from heaven onto your lap, and nothing will come to you from heaven automatically, **you will have to draw it by faith**. Please note, this statement is very important, without this **faith**, you will not be able to experience this "**unlimited returns**" from heaven that God promises in His word.

You cannot afford to be weak in **faith**; when it comes to matters of faith, do not consider your weaknesses, do not consider your status in life, do not look at yourself, do not even listen to what others say about you. These things breed unbelief and doubt in your mind, they weaken your faith; they keep your eyes downwards instead of upwards to God. You have to be fully convinced that the God, who has promised, is also able to perform that which He has promised. An open heaven is what God promises to give unto you. Jesus said: **'whatsoever things you desire'**, there is NO LIMIT.

Faith is that mental stamina conducive for a relationship with the 'Possessor of heaven and earth'. Faith is the only thing that will stabilise your mind and keep it focused on the truth of God no matter what is rocking your boat. Expect your faith in God to grow, one day at a time, just like in any other relationship. Your relationship with God will certainly grow. When your faith in Him grows, you'll be able to place more demands on Him by faith; that's when you can believe God to do greater works than before in your life.

God is with you in the dark as He is with you in the light of day, so learn how to live with little and how to live with much, for **God is always with you wherever you are and in whatever situation**; in the fire, in the flood, in the storm, in the pit, in prison, on the mountain, in the valley, whether you are happy or sad, in times of peace and in times of trouble, in times of joy and in times of sorrow. Fill your mind with thoughts of truth; it is that which makes you 'different' from the rest. As long as your MIND is firmly fixed on God, and knowing very well that He is able to save and to deliver you, God will have no choice but to keep your heart and mind in perfect peace. When you lie down to sleep, you will not be afraid, you will lie down and your sleep shall be sweet, for the Lord, "Possessor of heaven and earth" will make you dwell in safety.

This information alone is worth more than any amount of money you may have paid for this book. In a world where **Cause** and **Effect** is referred to as the 'iron law' of the universe, which will never change; and if like causes always produce like effects, then YOU MUST become SUCCESSFUL without fail, and NOBODY can put a limit on your success. No man can determine how successful you could be, no WITCHCRAFT can stop you; no force under the heavens can ever put you down. Your own experiences with God, "Possessor of heaven and earth", in this matter, will be the proof I give you.

Satan will do anything in his power to stop you from understanding this. **He is right by your side as you read this book**; if you still DO NOT UNDERSTAND the whole concept, then it is his duty to steal from you even the little understanding you may have grasped from reading this book. This is why I ask you to **read it again and again until you have grasped the truths in it**, and then you will become unstoppable.

REMEMBER THESE

1. It is a good thing to bring God your tithes, **it keeps your MIND fixed on God** as the TRUE SOURCE of ALL things, and it takes your MIND off others.
2. God invites all men to bring Him their tithes; by so doing you acknowledge that it is God who gives you power to get wealth, for in Him you live and in Him you move and in Him you have your being. The wise in heart will hear and understand and will respond to it.
3. Carefully adapt a system that will keep good records of your increase. The wise in heart will hear and understand and will be instructed.
4. God gets the **Glory and Honour** when you bring Him your Tithes and Offerings. This is **very, very important** to God, He MUST get glory for all the things done under the sun.
5. You get connected to God, and to his invisible and inexhaustible world of supply, and God gives you access to "an open heaven", giving you UNLIMITED RETURNS for responding to His INVITATION, in that, **whatsoever things** you desire, when you **pray, believe that you will receive them**, and **you shall have them**". And when you say unto this mountain, be thou removed, and be thou cast into the sea; and shall **not doubt** in your heart, but shall

believe that those things which you say **shall come to pass,** you **shall surely have whatsoever you say**.

Be confident in this one thing; as long as you remain in **right standing** with God, your thoughts will always be right, for God is in your thoughts. Whatever project God lays on your heart to fulfil, either big or small, go ahead and do it. Write it down, plan your course, commit it to God in prayer, and trust God to take you through your plans. Don't stop believing God that He is very well able to get you to your destination, only remain in right standing with Him. **Ignore any temporary failures**; let them be lessons to learn from. Many great men in history failed many times before they achieved success. Pay the price in full, ignore your critics, they've got time for what they do; just get busy with your plans, pay no attention to their words, do whatever it takes to accomplish your goals. Do not allow circumstances to shift your focus. Even if it means starting all over again, so be it, but don't give up, and you shall surely have the things your heart desires, just as God promised. It is God who has put His purposes in you and He's the one who seeks for you to succeed. God is very much interested in your success than you are, because He's got GLORY trapped in your success. For this reason you can trust Him to bring you to your desired destination.

You need not compare yourself to others, if you do so, you may never take the **first** step to achieve your goals. Remember, you are not in competition with any man; you only seek to pursue the desires of your heart. There is more than enough supply for everybody from the invisible world, so you need not fear. There are no shortages from where all things come from so don't rush for things. Do not believe the systems of the world; do not put your faith in them, for they depend on what their eyes can see that is why they hoard and compete for everything, to them there is not enough to go around for everyone. The world conditions your mind to believe that there is scarcity of resources, and there is not enough to go around for everybody, and when you BELIEVE this philosophy, you THINK and act in that manner, and you find yourself competing for everything in life; so you live your life in fear; you always want to beat people, you want to get ahead of people "by any means". This kind of philosophy is completely opposite to what exists in God's government, which is the Kingdom of God, where FAITH alone will get you WHATSOEVER THINGS your heart desires. Again, this piece of information alone is worth every penny you may have paid for this book.

As a result of your obedience to this invitation to return to God in the matter of Tithes and offerings as explained in this book, the grace of God will increase upon your life, and sooner than later, your own strength and ability will count for nothing. It will be too late for men to stop you, and when your goals are crystal clear, God will bring them to pass. How God will do it, you cannot tell, but men certainly cannot stop you.

When God's grace is fully at work in you, you don't need to explain to people, and they don't need to understand what is happening to you; even you yourself may not understand it fully. You and everyone else only need to co-operate with God to accomplish that which He has began in your life. When God's grace is fully at work in you, anybody who tries to fight you will only meet with frustration, for Gods grace makes no sense to the natural or carnal MIND.

Never mind what your condition or status may be today, and do not worry about your own strengths, or how weak you may be financially, physically or mentally. God's grace is able to carry you on wings like the eagle, to soar higher and higher in life daily. It is the grace of God that makes all the difference in one's life.

PLEASE MAKE NOTE OF THESE

1. There is but one original source where all things come from.

2. All others are resources, channels by which all things reach us.

3. Everyone must connect himself to this original source.

4. All things that are seen come from an invisible, inexhaustible world of things.

5. Unwavering faith will get you all things.

6. God is worthy to receive ALL glory.

7. God shares His GLORY with no man and no other god.

8. God is a jealous God; you hurt God's feelings when you give glory to all others but Him.

9. Withholding GLORY from God is robbing God. Why? Because God is the only One WORTHY to receive Glory.

10. Ascribe to God all the glory due to his name.

11. Giving God Tithes and Offerings is acknowledging that God is the source of your wealth, and this is an honourable thing to do.

12. Tithe is also an expression of love and gratitude to God. Love always expresses itself naturally through giving. God Himself seeks to have this one to one relationship with you, so He can express Himself fully in you, to will and to do of his good pleasure.

13. God Himself is the one seeking to reinstate this one-to-one relationship with man. If this were not important to God, He

would not have sought for it. "Return unto me and I will return unto you", says the Lord. It is God who wants to live in you and to fulfil all His purposes in you.

"Hear, O heavens, and give ear, O earth: for the LORD hath spoken, I have nourished and brought up children, and they have rebelled against me".
All we like sheep have gone astray; **we have turned every one to his own way**;
"**Come now, and let us reason together**, saith the LORD: though your sins be as scarlet, they shall be as white as snow; though they be red like crimson, they shall be as wool".
Remember the words of Solomon: 'fools hate knowledge; fools despise knowledge and instruction; the hearts of fools are void of understanding; a fool trusts in his own heart; the way of a fool is right in his own eyes.

14. It is God who worketh in you both to will and to do of His good pleasure. He wants to keep your mind alive by keeping it stayed and completely focused on Him. Seek God's purposes in all things; even in pain, his purposes must be sought.

15. Nobody is exempted in this beautiful relationship of bringing tithes and offerings to God; bringing Him Glory and honour; **even the priest must look up to God for all things**.

16. Ask God for Wisdom to make good the knowledge you have obtained in this book. Wisdom is the "power" to make good use of knowledge. Please do not take this lightly; people still pick up fines and points on their driving licences not because

they lack knowledge of the traffic laws or that they are not aware of the speed limits on the roads. There are a few doctors you may know who still smoke heavily and drink alcohol beyond the prescribed limits. There are pastors you know who fornicate and commit adultery, not because they lack the knowledge of the scriptures.

17. God will not take that which belongs to another man and give it to you. Rather God will cause men who have in their possession those things that you desire to locate you wherever you may be, but when they give you the things you desire you will in turn have to give to them the equivalent of the things they desire of you. In this way, you will never desire to have the things that belong to another man. All you really want in life is that which belongs to you. "Ask for your own DAILY BREAD"

18. As a man thinketh in his heart so is he. Man takes on the attitude of his thoughts. So if you think it is your own might that has gotten you your wealth, you take on that attitude, you become arrogant for you think it is your own strength and wisdom that has yielded these riches.

A QUESTION FOR YOU

If you came to me looking for 'everything', and if I gave you 'everything', what more would you be looking for? I'm sure your answer will be absolutely 'NOTHING', simply because I already gave you 'everything'.

I can assure you that, this ONE act of 'faithfully and reverently' bringing your Tithes and Offerings to God alone, with the understanding I have laid down in this book, will cause you to ALWAYS look upwards to God, the "possessor of heaven and earth", setting your **heart** and **mind** on Him, as the '**true source**' of all things; regarding all others as channels by which God meets all the desires of your heart. This should be your daily attitude towards God for the rest of your life.

Jesus said, you MUST look upwards to the Father in prayer for your 'DAILY BREAD', which includes all things that pertain to life and godliness, both physical and spiritual 'bread'. When you understand what you have just read, you would have solved life's puzzle; surely you will be heading towards SUCCESS in life.

The relationship you want to maintain throughout life is really the one between **YOU** and **"the source of all things"**. You will learn to have confidence in God gradually as your relationship grows each day. Your faith in Him will get stronger and stronger. **Nothing** will scare you in life any more. **Fear,** your greatest enemy to success, will be totally defeated, and nothing can stop you from achieving all your goals.

ANOTHER THING TO NOTE

When you make God the source of your supply, never mind what happens, stand firm, and **F**aith alone will turn everything around for you. How long are you supposed to hold on for? Well, do what Job did; hold on "**until your change comes**". This is the right and surest way to get anything you want from above. The Law of Attraction says this: you will **always** attract, positive or negative, people and circumstances that are in harmony with your **dominant** thoughts. That is to say, whatever you THINK about most of the time, you also attract into your life. It is important for you to be aware of this Mental Law, for it works for or against you 24 hours a day. This knowledge will help you filter the thoughts you allow to dominate your MIND. Here is where you apply the power of your free will, to make the choices of THOUGHTS necessary for those circumstances you want to invite into your life.

You have believed that there is ONE source from which all things proceeds and that is what you want to set your mind on. All you want to do is to relate yourself with this source in a **harmonious way**. If you keep thinking about God as the source of all things, then you will surely attract God to yourself. The effect of this way of thinking on your MIND is what's important. Your **faith will be in God** and in God alone. And if you are in business, you will be expecting God to bring clients to you, and you will NOT be afraid of what competitors do, for you are not in competition with them for YOUR clients. You will avoid cutting corners or corrupting yourself with all sorts of schemes and deception that goes on in other companies. Your faith will be firmly fixed on nothing else and on no other but on the source of all things; on God, the 'Adonai' Himself.

EVERY DAY MUST BE A SUCCESSFUL DAY

A successful day can be measured by the condition of **your STATE OF MIND** at the end of each day, which is a more important form than any other form of measure. Your state of mind at the end of each day will reveal how **HAPPY** you really are and how **FULFILLED** you truly are at the end of each day. TODAY is more important than TOMORROW, for you only have today, you do not have tomorrow yet. If you or anybody wants to measure your success, you can only measure it up to TODAY. When your trust is in God daily, your mind is at rest in Him, no matter what happens to you in the day. You go through each day with your **MIND** firmly fixed on Him, expecting all things to come from Him; everyone else will be a mere channel God chooses to use for the day.

If you do this, you will never look to man for anything and your heart will not be broken by disappointments from men, for you expect nothing from men, only from God. Men are here today, dead tomorrow. How sure can you be, that the man who promised you a job today will be alive tomorrow? But if you **fix your MIND on God** for all the things you expect in that day, God is OBLIGED to keep your MIND in perfect peace because you TRUST Him. Whoever He chooses to be of a blessing to you in any day is up to God. And you will not be expecting that person to be there for you tomorrow, because God can decide to choose someone else.

RESOLVE to make everyday a SUCCESSFUL DAY, by so doing you will be mindful of **EVERYTHING** that comes your way to make each day a SUCCESSFUL DAY, also so that you will be THANKFUL for ALL THINGS. Every little thing that helps you on your way will be **ACKNOWLEDGED**, NOTHING TAKEN FOR GRANTED.

It is my strongest belief that '**Every day**' is the **best way** to measure how successful you BECOME. Here's why:

1. You set out each day with clear goals FOR THE DAY, and clearly lay out definite plans to achieve them in that day. Doing all that can be done in A DAY. Leaving tomorrow's work for tomorrow.
2. It reduces stress; for you will not have to 'kill' yourself trying to do tomorrow's work today.
3. You are able to correct your mistakes daily, not leaving vital corrections for too long, especially the necessary corrections in your attitudes.
4. You will be able to enjoy everyday and be Thankful for Everyday when the day's work is done. There are many more advantages you will discover in your own experiments.

When you make the "Possessor of heaven and earth", the strength of your life, you will no longer be afraid of the **threats** posed by **ordinary men**, but your confidence and security will be in God; and that He is well able to save and deliver you even at the point of death.

When your MIND is constantly **fixed on God** as your SOURCE, and when you make all men mere channels by which God gets the blessings to you, then you can boldly look to the heavens and say:

> **"My help comes from the Lord, the maker of heaven and earth.**
> The LORD shall preserve me from all evil
> The Lord shall preserve my soul.
> The LORD shall preserve my going out and my coming in from this time forth, and even forevermore.
> God is my refuge and strength, a very present help in trouble.
> Therefore I will not fear, even though the earth be removed, and though the mountains be carried into the midst of the sea; though its waters roar and be troubled, though the mountains shake with its swelling.
> My help is in the name of the LORD, who made heaven and earth.

You will only be dealing with the **highest authority first** in all things, and that is God, in whom you have put your trust. Now, if this is not "**Unlimited Returns**" for your efforts, I wonder what is.

SELF-PITY

In this beautiful relationship you are about to forge with God, your past does not matter any more. Do not consider your background; not even the colour of your skin; it doesn't matter whether you were born black or white; never mind if you come from a poor family. Simply put: don't feel sorry for yourself, no matter what, and do not practice self-pity in your mind, don't join the 'pity party club'.

Self-pity is a useless, degrading, God-offending, debasing, soul-destroying practice. Do not allow yourself to be pulled into it; do not let people refer you to the past; it has a negative effect on your **mind**. Self-pity sets your mind on the wrong path, on the things you lack in yourself and on your weaknesses, instead of fixing your mind on God, the source of all things, who is more than able to bring you all the things you desire, either by men or from His invisible world of inexhaustible supply, where all things come from. Jesus warns: do not worry about tomorrow, for tomorrow will worry about itself.

People who worry about tomorrow never enjoy today. They are always stressed. They get stress related illnesses, which costs them a fortune. But it shall not be so with you.

DO NOT WORRY ABOUT TOMORROW

The fear of tomorrow is a 'killer'. It terrifies you even before you go to bed at night. This fear is made worse when the resources you have today does not seem to be enough for the plans you have made for tomorrow. The fear of tomorrow leaves a negative effect on your mind, it shoots arrows of doubts and fear into your mind and thoughts, and these doubts move you farther away from God. God will not allow any man to doubt Him. He has nothing more to prove to this world than He has already done.

In this special relationship with God, you must live life one day at a time, never to worry about tomorrow. **Do not think about tomorrow** today, that is to say, deal with tomorrow's business tomorrow. This is the only way to overcome the fear of tomorrow today. Get rid of the thoughts of tomorrow from your mind completely. Remove tomorrow and all its schedules from your mind. Never think about tomorrow or anything that pertains to another day. The thoughts of anything that is supposed to happen tomorrow or any other day must not occupy your mind today. The only way to do that, since you cannot leave your mind empty is to substitute the thoughts of tomorrow or any other day with thoughts of today. Concentrate only on today. Think about goals you have set out to achieve today. You cannot be troubled by the fear of tomorrow if you **never** think about them. How you achieve your goals tomorrow is none of your business, God knows what's coming tomorrow, He knows the troubles of tomorrow, and He knows how to take you through every day successfully, that is your faith in Him.

Pilots understand this better; when they make their plans for their trips, they simply hand it over to the people on the ground. When they start the engines of the plane and begin to fly in the air, they cannot see above or below them, they cannot tell for sure what the circumstances in the air will be like, neither can they anticipate the sudden changes in the weather conditions, in fact they cannot tell what is about to happen in the skies, yet they rest their minds, trusting in the ability and expertise of the men on the ground to direct them safely to their destinations. So God will keep your mind in perfect peace unless you allow the thoughts of tomorrow to enter your mind today. Nothing shall by any means cause you to fear tomorrow if you learn to live your life one day at a time.

WHATEVER YOU DWELL UPON IN YOUR MIND GROWS

You give life to the things you think about. Whatever you don't think about leaves the mind, because your conscious mind can only hold one thought at a time. The more you think about a thing, the more life you give it in your mind, and the more life you give a thing, the more it grows, and the more it grows in your mind, the more you worry about it, the more you worry the more fear grips your heart with all its associated diseases, and those diseases may cut short your life. Nothing is solved by worry; in fact it has no usefulness at all. It is the devil's weapon to disturb your mind for when your mind is sick, your whole being cannot function well.

YOUR MIND AND YOUR BELIEF SYSTEM

Jesus said: "and when you pray, do not use vain repetitions as the heathen do. For they **think** that they will be heard for their many words. Have you been to a place recently where people do that, repeating themselves because they '**believe**' by so doing they will be heard?

Upon this word '**believe**' alone, hangs all our attitudes, not only in prayer. A young girl commits abortion because she **believes** the child she is carrying is 'not human yet'. A young boy wants to become a girl because he **believes** 'he is a girl trapped in a boy's body'. A rich man loses millions in business and then he goes to hang himself, committing suicide because he **believes** he cannot cope with the situation, he believes it is better for him to end his life than live to see another day. A man **believes** he is superior to another man because of his race or the colour of his skin, so he treats other people who are not like him with contempt, as if they were less humans. Is this not the kind of '**belief**' that produces poisonous substances such as racism, prejudice and the like in the minds of people? If what you believe is therefore a lie, you may be building your entire life upon the foundation of lies.

GUARD YOUR MIND WITH ALL DILIGENCE

All the thousands of TV stations, radio stations, the internet, newspapers, magazines, advertising boards and all the different forms of media out there are after your mind; everybody is trying to get something into your mind, and God is no different. God, through this book is also seeking the attention of your MIND.

If you get the mind of a man, you get the whole man. When information reaches your subconscious mind, it stays there forever, it becomes part of you, and the press knows exactly how to do this very well. They repeat things over and over; they keep feeding your mind relentlessly. Most people do not understand the **serious assaults** on their minds each day as they go about their normal lives.

We are spiritual beings, and as spiritual beings we must not go after the effects that we see happening in our lives, we must deal with their spiritual causes. Every effect is as a result of a cause we may not see; thoughts in our minds, whether they be good or bad.

Ignorance of this device of the enemy is an automatic loss in your fight for a victorious and successful life. Paul says, even though we walk in the flesh, we do not war after the flesh. That is to say, you do not deal with the physical effects in your life, which are those things that you attract to yourself as a result of the thoughts in your mind, rather you deal with the cause, which are the unseen thoughts in your mind that invite these effects to come into your life; you kind of invite them to yourself freely by the way you think. As a thinking being, you give life to the things you think about, whether they be good or bad, and they will always manifest themselves in the physical realm.

Power over your own mind therefore, is power over circumstances. The things you allow or permit to enter your own mind, are the things that affect you. If you can GUARD your mind with all diligence, you will be in control of what affects you and or what doesn't. The things that never reach your mind do not affect you; for example, you will shed no tears if you never hear about the death of a very good friend of yours, even though you love that friend dearly.

Therefore guard your heart with all diligence, for out of it are the issues of life. Be mindful of the things you allow to enter your MIND, for when they settle in your subconscious mind, they influence you in every way; in your thoughts and actions. Mind the things you see and hear and touch or feel daily, for by repetition, a thing is formed in your subconscious mind and stays there forever until change comes. The things you see with your eyes and hear with the ears can influence you greatly so guard your eyes and ears with all diligence. Filter the things you allow through these gates. Consider the power of the internet, television, radio, smart mobile phones, newspapers, magazines, etc., and how they influence your MIND through this media. Again I urge you to protect your subconscious mind by filtering information that reaches you via the eyes and ears.

Rich men protect their treasured possessions with all their might; your **mind is worth all the protection you can give it.** Your MIND is worth more than the palaces of kings or the vaults of banks. If you value your mind that much, you will accord it all the security it needs. A great man called Job, understood this **truth**, and made a covenant with his eyes and said to himself: henceforth, **I will NOT corrupt my MIND by looking at a young woman lustfully.** You too can instruct the members of your body to do likewise.

THE POWER IS WITHIN YOU

This then is how you use the weapons of spiritual warfare: do what Jesus did, by **suggesting the right thoughts to your MIND.** Replace the negative thoughts in your mind with the right thoughts. The law of substitution will always work for you in this matter. These negative thoughts are the fiery darts of the enemy shot at you, with the aim to mess your mind up daily, to weaken your faith. For when they capture your mind, they get your whole being. When you start thinking negative thoughts you attract the manifestation of these thoughts to yourself in the physical realm; it is a law of the mind, where there is a cause therefore, there must be an effect, and that is what you see coming into your life. So don't just say I cast down this thought, or I cast this negative thought out of my mind, it is not enough; rather suggest the right thoughts to your mind and start thinking about that instead. It is like just standing there in the dark and complaining about the darkness in your room. The right thing to do is turn on the light and darkness will flee. Turn on the heaters, and the cold temperature will vanish. So do what Jesus did, say, "It is written" and then suggest the right thoughts to your mind. Paul said, "whatsoever things are true, honest, just, pure, lovely, of good report, if there be any virtue, if there be any praise, THINK on these things. This is how you defeat and destroy the works of the devil in your mind, for Christ was made manifest, to reveal TRUTH unto us, so we can **think right**, and by so doing destroy and pull down strongholds of the enemy in our minds, the very cause of the sins that easily beset us; bringing into captivity every thought to the obedience of Christ, casting down every evil imagination in your mind and any thought that is not in agreement with the Word of God.

Remember God cares for your body as much as He cares for your soul, that's why He still provides healing for your body, to keep you here, until your work on earth is accomplished. You are only useful to God on earth in the body, that's why you MUST maintain holiness, to keep attracting God to yourself; for the Spirit of God only dwells **continually** in holy vessels. Consequently, entertaining impure thoughts in your mind will attract the likes to you. By law you are always attracting to yourself people and circumstances that are in harmony with the thoughts you permit your mind to think about daily, whether you know about this mental law or not. So when the enemy plants a thought in your mind which is not in harmony with the Word of God, quickly root that thought out of your mind by replacing it with the right thoughts from the Word of God. The wise in heart will hear and understand and will be instructed.

For the young man who is still struggling with thoughts of sexual impurity in the mind, CAST those thoughts from your mind: say out loud to yourself: "do you not know that you are the temple of God and that the Spirit of God dwells in you"? If any man defile the temple of God, him shall God destroy, for the temple of God is holy, which **YOU ARE!**

These few words may sound simple, but I tell you the truth, they have **power** to bring into captivity such impure thoughts to the obedience of Christ. Be your own therapist, administer it to yourself and see the results for yourself. If you shut your mouth, those impure thoughts will gain root in your mind and will overcome you. *Oh young man, remember that, sin lies at your door, and its desire is for you, BUT YOU SHOULD RULE OVER IT!!!*

A WORD TO FATHERS

One good thing a father can leave his children for an everlasting possession is to teach them to fix their MINDS on God, their heavenly Father. When a father is no more, his children will be fine, for their heavenly Father will always be there for them, He never dies, and He will never leave them nor forsake them; He will be with them every second of the time. He's never short of supplies, and He will withhold nothing good from them.

When king David was about to die, he called his son Solomon and he spoke to him saying: "my son, as for me, it was in my mind to build an house unto the name of the LORD my God, but the word of the LORD came to me, saying, I shall not build an house unto the name of the Lord, but a son shall be born to me, his name shall be Solomon, and I will give peace and quietness unto Israel in his days, he shall build an house for the name of the LORD; and **he shall be my son, and I will be his Father**; and I will establish the throne of his kingdom over Israel for ever". Wow, what a word to hear from the mouth of a dying father. In other words, David was telling his son, I am about to die, but you will not be left fatherless for God Himself will be your Father even when I'm dead and gone.

It is important to note that, God associates the word "Father" to Himself, because He is the source of all things. He is the founder of everything; He established all things. He is the source of all things, and He also is the ONE who sustains all things. An understanding of this truth will give you and your children confidence in your relationship with the Father in heaven, and you will live a worry-free life. Truly, in Him we live, and in Him we move and in Him we have our being. He is God, our Father.

It is every earthly father's duty to exemplify to his children the love and care our heavenly Father has for us, and to register these thoughts in the minds of his children permanently. For as long as his children remain under his care, from the day they are born till the day they leave home to join their husbands or wives in holy matrimony, they will never have to worry about what they will eat or what they will drink, or what they will wear, neither do they have to worry about the basic necessities of life.

As a father, you must groom your children to have this understanding in their minds, so when they leave home as adults, they will have the same mindset towards their heavenly Father, who is the true Father, even though He cannot be seen.

Your real duty as an earthly father is to fix the minds of your children on their heavenly Father. You must keep pointing the FATHER to them; let it be firmly registered in their minds, so that the day they leave your home, it will just be like you are handing them over to their true Father. Having finished your work with them, they would have understood what it feels like to have a Father who cares.

No child should leave his father's house having no knowledge at all about his Heavenly Father. Many adults leave their fathers' homes, having no understanding, no knowledge, no relationship whatsoever with their heavenly Father. So they go out there struggling to survive everyday. They worry about what to eat, what to drink, what to wear etc., worst of all, they keep worrying about TOMORROW.

I hope by now it will be easy for you to understand why a child is commanded by the law of the only WISE God to '**honour**' his father and mother. You see, when you bring God, your heavenly Father, your tithes and offerings, you actually **honour** Him, you pay tribute to Him, you show Him the high respect you have for Him, you speak well of Him, and you make Him feel good.

The principle is the same for your earthly father and mother as it is for God, and so it is in the child's own interest to honour his father and mother, for the benefits thereof are more than money can buy. Here is the promise: that 'IT MAY BE WELL WITH YOU; that you may live long in the land of the living'. Is this not '**unlimited returns**' for your obedience? Let me emphasise this point: I know a few rich men who died because the doctors could not cure them of their diseases. Not that they could not pay for their medical bills; they wished to live a little longer, but their money couldn't buy them long life. Again, nobody MUST live without a 'father'; if your earthly father fails you, quickly connect yourself to your 'Heavenly Father'. He will NEVER FAIL you, and He really cares for you.

People who do not put themselves under the care of their Heavenly Father worry about things, they choke themselves with the cares and riches and pleasures of this life. They carry on their shoulders all the burdens of life; what a stressful way to live your life.

I strongly believe that one of the reasons why Jesus showed up on earth, was to bring back the 'consciousness' and the knowledge of our 'Heavenly Father' into our minds, and to restore that relationship we first had with Him as 'Father and son'. No good thing will the Father withhold from them that maintain their right standing with Him.

When your mind is set on God, even healing flows through your physical body. It is all about the fixing of your mind on God. He will keep in perfect peace, whose mind is stayed on Him, that's a sure PROMISE.

GIVING TO THE POOR

Let us talk a little about giving offerings to the poor and needy. Herein is another way that you can give to God. When you give to the poor and needy, you lend to God, for they too are God's children. A little caution here: not that you make it your business to feed the poor in the world, because you cannot do that, you don't even have enough resources to do so, neither can you reach all the poor in the world. Do not attempt to make it your full time job to eradicate poverty in the world, especially in the way most Charity companies go about it. Most of these Charities have their own agendas, which have very little to do with the people they claim they want to help.

Every man has been given power exclusively over his own will and MIND; Jesus said: you will always have the poor with you: there is a very good reason why He said that. First, reach the ones closer to you, especially the poor and needy in your household and in your family, in your neighbourhood, in your church, in your community, in your city, in your own country, before you attempt to reach the world.

Please note, when you give to the poor and needy, you should not do it with the intention of eradicating poverty; you cannot eradicate poverty by giving handouts to the poor, for the poor must decide for themselves the change they want in their lives. It is the **unchanged mindset** that keeps a man in poverty. Having little today DOES

NOT mean you are poor, but if you THINK you are POOR, then you are. It is the way you THINK that keeps you poor or rich. Most self-made millionaires started with NOTHING, but they didn't see themselves as poor, they never THOUGHT like the poor, so they eventually became rich.

Remember to GIVE TO THE POOR and NEEDY, for you lend to God when you give to them. Great men in history had always given generously to God, especially in the act of giving to the poor and needy. The psalmist asked: "what is man that you are so mindful of him"? Think about this for a minute: you see, God is always about man's business here on earth. I believe God is so consumed with the thoughts of man everyday. His love for us is strong and his faithfulness towards us is eternal. The sun still shines upon us, the rain still falls every year, the sea is not allowed to pass its borders, the air is still free for all etc. Look how much God so love the world; He would rather have all men to be saved and to come to the knowledge of the truth.

I encourage individuals, businesses, companies, churches and every organisation to bring their Tithes to God. This will produce more Faith in you towards God than ever before and your expectations of God will become faith, and Faith alone is all you need to get you "whatsoever things you desire" in life without sweat.

Companies that respond to this call by bringing their tithes to God will be submitting themselves and their entire organisation under the mighty influence of God; and the faith of the leadership of these companies will be in God, not in the markets. However strong the markets may be, no matter the stability of the economy in your country, it is always better to trust in the Lord, (the possessor of heaven and earth) than to put confidence in man or in systems. Blessed is the nation whose God is the Lord.

You will never fear competition and you will never be in haste to get wealth. Your mind and that of the leaders of organisations will rather be fixed on the source of all things, and this effect on the MIND is what's more important, it is the KEY to SUCCESS. All successful people have a different mentality, they THINK differently, and this mindset makes them stand out from the rest.

When the effect of this begins to show in you and in the work of your hands, people will draw near to you, just to find out from you, 'what exactly is the secret to your prosperity'. When they come, do not hesitate to show them the way.

EVERYBODY MUST BRING GLORY TO GOD

Every one under the sun, including Men of God who stand in God's place to receive tithes, companies, sole proprietors, individuals, etc, MUST bring their tithes unto God; for ALL MUST continually look up to God for all their needs. Every **mind** must be fixed on God at all times, and all must see others as channels God chooses to use to get all things to them. ALL must continually acknowledge that God is their source, from whom all things come, and ALL must continually give thanks to God for the things they receive. All peoples MUST set their minds on Him as the ORIGINAL source from where all good and perfect things come.

Leaders of Ministries and local churches must also do this honourable thing, because all MUST put their faith in God, not in the membership of local churches. The membership of the local church cannot finance the "**great projects**" God lays on the hearts of great Ministers. They must always put their faith and trust in God to accomplish great works for God. Leaders who compare their ministries to smaller ministries make a big mistake; you have no idea the potential that still remains unfolded in you. The measure of success you CAN ACHIEVE cannot compare with the measure of success you may have already attained. Remember, whatever brought you here must keep you going. The fact that you still have breath in you is evident that there is still more you can achieve for God in your lifetime. You cannot afford to rely on church membership to get your projects done. You have come too far in the Lord to depend on people now; it doesn't matter how large your congregation may be today.

This is what will happen to the minds of individuals and even board of directors, managers and owners of businesses that give tithes to God; they will be looking upwards to God continually for MORE; their faith will be in God continually no matter what happens, they will look to God for more ideas, for more investors, for more talented workers, for more clients, for more customers and for more resources they do not know about yet. Their faith will be in God not in the markets or in economic policies of governments. Blessed is the nation whose God is the Lord (the Possessor of heaven and earth).

This idea may sound strange or too religious to you, but consider, the things you already have, came from God, (the possessor of heaven and earth). All the resources of the earth both natural and human resources from which all companies and nations benefit, was deposited on earth by Him. He owns the earth and all the things in it: the fertile lands, the sea, the air we breathe for life, the fishes in the sea, the gold, silver and precious metals, the diamonds, the oil, the farm lands etc; all belongs to Him. Again I say, "Blessed is the nation whose God is the Lord".

God is looking forward to the nation who will bring Him honour and glory; He is looking forward to individuals and businesses that will honour Him and bring Him glory by the giving of Tithes and Offerings, as a result of understanding the principles laid down in this book. Every nation must bring GLORY to God, because He deserves

ALL the glory and honour and power. God MUST get GLORY from everyone and for everything done under the sun.

Leaders of nations that dare prove God (the Possessor of Heaven and earth) by bringing Him glory, will surely have "access to an open heaven", where all things come from, for the benefit of the nation they rule. And 'whatsoever' things they desire as a nation, according to the will of God, they can confidently approach God in prayer, present their petitions to Him, believing that their petitions have been heard and granted, and looking forward to the manifestation of the things they have asked for, and with earnest faith their expectations will never be cut off; they will surely get what they have asked for, no matter how long it takes.

People do not give God the glory because they do not acknowledge Him as the source of the things they have received. People withhold gratitude and glory, which belongs to God and they rather give thanks to other gods or to men for the things they receive, and so **they ROB God of the glory which belongs to Him**. If you understand this, you can't help but to Honour God with your tithes and offerings, and you will do so with all reverence. Not only will you honour God with your tithes and offerings but with everything you do with your life, and for everything you achieve in life.

IN A NUT SHELL

Bringing your Tithes and Offerings unto God must be with the attitude of Gratitude and with the UNDERSTANDING of who God is, (as He is the Possessor of heaven and earth); not under compulsion by Law, but by your own volition, motivated by your LOVE for God. You must freely and willingly give unto God, a TENTH of all your increase and offerings too as an investment in the Kingdom of God, and God shall surely bless you.

I do not know yet how Abraham arrived at the figure 1/10 (one tenth), for He was the first man to give one-tenth of all to the king of Righteousness. However, God Himself approved of this figure, for He made it a law unto the nation of Israel, the descendants of Abraham, whom He has chosen among the nations of the world, to keep for an ordinance forever, and he set men aside to receive Tithes and Offerings on His behalf.

The essence of law is to create culture. So God first made giving of Tithes a law to the nation of Israel after He delivered them with an outstretched arm from Egypt. God intended to cause them to LEARN to relate to Him, in the area of 'giving and receiving', but the only way to cause them to give back to God was to make it a law, because they did not know Him well. The nation of Israel could not relate to God (the "Possessor of heaven and earth") in the same manner as their father Abraham did, because they did not know Him very well, let alone express their PROFOUND LOVE towards Him by WILLINGLY giving Him a Tenth of all their increase. The only way God could cause them to do so was to make giving of 'Tithes' a law, and they were obliged under the law to bring the Tithes and Offerings to God, and by so doing God created in them the habit of GIVING, forming in the nation of Israel the culture of giving to God, by 'Tithes and Offerings'.

It is important to note that, the laws we allow in a nation create the culture in that nation. So for example, if homosexuality becomes a law in any nation, people can go to court to demand justice with regards to that part of the law if they were discriminated against. It also means, it will be 'NORMAL PRACTICE' to see one male and another male, or a female and another female kissing passionately in public. There will be no culture SHOCK at all, because that too becomes part of the culture.

Culture cannot hide itself; it is the first thing you will identify with the people when you enter into a new environment. It is displayed among the people everywhere; it is enshrined in the subconscious minds of the people and they live and express it freely and openly. It is like everybody going about saying 'silently': THIS IS WHAT WE DO HERE, and THIS IS HOW WE DO IT!

The KEY to life is UNDERSTANDING, once you understand what I have shared with you here in this book, you too will be able to relate yourself with THE SOURCE of ALL THINGS in a HARMONIOUS WAY. Your lifestyle of GIVING and RECEIVING will be with a difference. A new **MIND** and a new **HEART** shall come to you, and with a GRATEFUL heart, you too can relate yourself to God, the source of ALL things. It will be 'normal practice' to you to bless God at all times, and to express unto Him a DEEP and PROFOUND GRATITUDE in all things.

Everyday, your attitude towards God when you are about to give Him your 'Tithes and Offerings' will be like this: 'O Lord God, our Father, all that I have came from you; it is a privilege to give back to you part of what You have given to me. You are my source forever, thank you Lord'. This kind of attitude, will keep your MIND fixed on God daily as your source, never looking to man as your source, but only as channels bywhich God reaches you.

When you bring yourTithes and Offerings to God, you **acknowledge** that God is the source of the things you have already received and that He gave you the ability to acquire them. Secondly, giving Tithes and Offerings serve as a **tangible reminder** to you, that everything you possess belongs to God and you are but a faithful steward. The **effect** of this **on your mind** is very important, because it keeps your **MIND** connected to the source of true riches at all times. This means you can always look up to God for more. The more you become aware of this truth, the more it draws your **mind** into a closer touch with God, the source of everything you will ever need in life.

If you do this consistently and reverently as worship unto God, your special relationship with God will get stronger. You will cease from begging or looking elsewhere for help, God Himself will be a very present help in time of trouble, for He is closer to you than a brother. Your help comes from God not men; He will use men, but He is the one helping you. When you understand this, you will always give

glory to God for all things, for you will clearly see His Hands at work for your good in ALL things, because you have set your love upon Him. This is the kind of **mindset** I bring to you in this book. This is the kind of relationship I want you to establish with God, the source of ALL things, the "Possessor of heaven and earth".

God is KING, and He created us in His image as kings on earth, to have dominion over all that He has put here on earth, to rule the earth for Him as His sons and daughters. It is important to note that, the words of the king become law, even unto the king himself. God is holy as King because He holds Himself to His words; He fulfils His words, and He always does what he says He will do. If God is holy and is a God of INTEGRITY, then His sons and daughters MUST be holy too.

However, the ULTIMATE GOAL of God with regards to His laws and His relationship with man is this: it is God's intention to "put His laws in our MINDS and to write them on our hearts, and all men shall KNOW God, from the least to the greatest among men. The Holy Spirit who dwells in us will lead us into ALL TRUTH and He will do this work in us. It won't be long, nobody is going to need a preacher to tell him to know God, or give to God their 'Tithes and Offerings', for the Holy Spirit will inspire all to do so.

Giving of Tithes and Offerings is ONE OF THE MOST BEAUTIFUL ways to relate to God. Solomon says, "HONOUR the Lord with your possessions, and with the first fruits of all your increase". It is not just about giving God a portion of your money, but you are supposed to HONOUR God with it; do it reverently, as a form of worship. Do it with all your heart and MIND. Hear what God says concerning His glory:

"I am the LORD: that is my name:
and my glory will I not give to another,
neither my praise to graven images".

Let me say that again in other words: God says, I am the OWNER of EVERYTHING, and nobody shares in my glory, the glory is all mine, all GLORY must be directed to me, and to me ALONE.

It is for this reason I have written this book, and when you understand the contents in this book, you too will have the privilege of joining the millions of people on the face of the earth who bring glory to God the Father, Creator of the heavens and the earth, by bringing your tithes and offerings unto God from time to time.

The only way God gets the GLORY in your tithes and offerings is by doing so reverently, from **your heart** with understanding and with your **mind completely focused** on what you are doing. **ALL GLORY** belongs to God for He is the 'King of Glory'. It is the **GLORY** God requires in your Tithes and Offerings, NOT YOUR MONEY!

God is inviting you to Himself, so you too can bring him **the GLORY due to His name** as you reverently bring Him your Tithes and Offerings. In return, He will give you an 'open access' to His invisible and inexhaustible world of supplies, from where all the things that are seen come from.

The offering of Cain and Abel unto God was about the **condition of their hearts and minds**, not about the things they gave for sacrifice. The condition of your heart is what determines the quality of what you offer to God. It is really about the INTANGIBLE factors of GRATITUDE AND HONOUR, and of giving GLORY to God for all your increase that matters most in this **special relationship** you are about to forge with God.

The ULTIMATE LAW of God is LOVE, all other laws lead you to LOVE, and Love has NO OPPRESSION whatsoever. Your GIVING of Tithes and Offerings MUST be motivated by your LOVE for God and NOTHING ELSE. You are establishing a **special relationship** between yourself and God, "Possessor of heaven and earth", the source from which all things proceed, on the FOUNDATION of LOVE. Everything you do in His name from today MUST be done because of your LOVE for Him, and nothing else. God Himself is Love, and He wants to fill you with Himself daily, so that whatever you do, will be MOTIVATED by LOVE, not by compulsion. You want God to be pleased with your 'giving', not for men to praise you for how generous you are.

Again God is the King of GLORY, and He has made us kings and rulers over the earth, so you must be like Him, and you must also act like Him. Here's how a King talks (and I'm referring to the King of Glory, the King of kings):

> "I will make you a great nation"
> "I will bless you and make your name great, and you shall be a blessing"

"I will bless those who bless you, and I will curse him who curses you"

"And in you all the families of the earth shall be blessed."

When Kings speak like this, they also HOLD THEMSELVES TO THEIR WORDS. When King Herod promised with an oath to give to the daughter of Herodias "*whatever she might ask*", king Herod had to hold himself to his words, so that even when the girl said to him, "give me John the Baptist's head on a platter", the king could not refuse her, so he sent and had John beheaded in prison because **he had spoken with his mouth**, and his words are very important to him.

In the same way, in this special relationship you are about to establish with God, you must be careful to treat your words as a king. When you speak with your mouth or say anything quietly to yourself even in your MIND, like: "this is what I will do for the Lord", **please hold yourself to it and do it**.

Here is a good place to start, especially if you have very little or NOTHING, you can draw near to God in prayer right now and say: "Our Father in heaven, Possessor of heaven and earth, "of all that **You** give me **I** will surely give a tenth to You."

First, give the very best of yourself to God; that is to say, give your best gift to God. There is no better gift to give God than your own life, this also include giving your life wholly to God and working daily to fulfil your purpose on earth; to unfold the all potential God has placed in you before you die. Also, give the best of your substance to God.

Love is expressed in giving, it is impossible to love and not give. When you are motivated by true love, **you will never waste another day of your life** on earth, because you want to give the best of yourself to God. You must take the least of every opportunity that presents itself in a day, to develop yourself, in order to unfold the good qualities hidden in you, and serve yourself to the world as a 'sweet smelling' offering to God, the ultimate offering that pleases Him.

Let me give you an example of giving, motivated by LOVE, and exemplified by God Himself:

> "For God SO LOVED the world that He gave His
> only begotten Son,
> that whoever believes in Him should not perish but
> have everlasting life".

Please note that, "love seems to be foolish"; because LOVE will make you give £100,000.00 as your Tithes to God from your net earnings of a £1,000,000.00 (one million pounds). Investment Bankers may describe you as a fool because they have a thousand ways of investing that kind of money for you.

YOUR PLEDGE TO GOD

Now I urge you to make a declaration with your mouth today, just like Jacob, and say with me:

> "Our Father in heaven, of ALL that You give me from today,
> **I will surely give a tenth to You**"

I can assure you that, your experience on this journey to 'unlimited returns' will be even better if YOU HAVE NOTHING to start with, so that you can start looking upwards to God for ALL the things that you desire, and when He gives them to you, hold yourself to your own words like a king, and honour your pledge to God. Make your words so important to you than anything else; honour your promises to God and let this beautiful relationship continue to the very end of your life, and it shall be well with you.

CONCLUSION

In writing this book, I have done my part, what you decide to do with it is up to you now. May you discover a lot more in God; enjoy your friendship with Him.

Finally, tell others about it, or recommend this book to them, lead them to God, the source of your own riches and let them discover for themselves the joy, the happiness, the stress-free life that you have obtained.

Again, please hear the words of **the source** of ALL THINGS: a statement of psychological truth: **"Return unto me, and I will return unto you"**.

In what shall we return, you may ask? **"In Tithes and Offerings"**.

Draw near to God, and He will draw near to you.

BONUS MATERIAL

Home Sweet Home

Home Sweet Home is a book I am writing for those who want a deeper relationship with God, a much better relationship than the one we have discussed in the book "Unlimited Returns". Surely, God will not despise anyone who brings Him the glory that is due to His name, by the giving of your tithes and offerings, acknowledging that He has given you the power to make wealth. Acknowledging that the things you have received so far, have come from Him, regardless of whether you are a member of a church or not. The Lord of heaven and earth says: "The one who comes to Me, I will by no means cast out.

If you keep looking upwards towards Him for all the things you desire, having faith in God, keeping your mind stayed on Him at all times, He will surely meet you at the point of your need. God will never disappoint anyone great or small if they look up to Him for all their needs with earnest faith, without a shadow of doubt in their minds, as we have already established in the book "Unlimited Returns".

But there is an even better and a more special relationship you may forge with God that I have not told you about yet. God is not just able to give you whatsoever things your heart desires, He also wants to be your Father again, and in fact this desire of God is even more important to Him. He is not only the source of all the things you need for life, HE IS ACTUALLY THE SOURCE and SUSTAINER OF LIFE itself.

You wonder why God wants too much of you now. I'm not asking you to join any religious group, most of them claim to know Him but they don't. Most of the people in these religious groups are very dedicated members of their religious organisations, but they do not have any relationship at all with the Father. This is not what the Father is seeking for; He doesn't want you to join a religious group, not at all. He only wants you to be restored to Him as His child again, that's all He wants.

Records have been carefully kept for our sakes, so we don't have to scratch everywhere looking for proof of God. The Bible will be just one source I will give you as proof of the existence of God, and all things God claims to be. Better still, God Himself will give you an infallible proof in many ways, just to prove to you that He is very much alive, and you will be more than satisfied with your own experience.

Some religious people may tell you that you are a sinner because of the bad things you have been doing, and that's why you need God. No, not at all. You are not a sinner because you sinned; NO! You were born a sinner even before you sucked your mother's milk. Before you committed the first wilful sin, none of your righteousness could please God. It is the 'nature of Adam' in you that makes you a sinner, not the sins you committed. It is impossible for the nature of sin to bear the fruits of righteousness, that's why every man needs help.

This is the only reason why you need to come back to God and be restored to the ONE ORIGINAL LIFE. He has made provisions for that, so if you want to know more, I invite you to find out for yourself. You will be glad you did.

If you happen to attend Church Service every Sunday, or you read the Bible by yourself at home daily, and none of these experiences bring you to the **Holy Spirit** or the Holy Spirit into you, I'm afraid you still haven't got the real thing yet. You don't want to remain in religion all the days of your life. Remember, most religious people are very good people, the only problem here is this: being religious does not make one a son of God, or a citizen of the Kingdom of God. The sons of God have the Holy Spirit residing in them and He leads them daily in the way to go.

A seven year old girl after her conversations with friends at school; she came to me and asked this question: "if a person calls himself a Christian and does not go to church, is he still a Christian? Now, this seven-year-old girl is too young to understand 'everything', but she recognises that there is much more to it than calling oneself a 'Christian'; as if the word 'Christian' was a **special title** to your name.

If you desire to know more, I recommend that you read the book "Home Sweet Home", which will soon be published.